10-11

LEAVING THE LEFT

LEAVING THE LEFT

Moments in the News That Made Me Ashamed to Be a Liberal

KEITH THOMPSON

SENTINEL

SENTINEL
Published by the Penguin Group
Penguin Group (USA) Inc., 375 Hudson Street, New York, New York 10014, U.S.A.
Penguin Group (Canada), 90 Eglinton Avenue East, Suite 700, Toronto, Ontario,
Canada M4P 2Y3 (a division of Pearson Penguin Canada Inc.)
Penguin Books Ltd, 80 Strand, London WC2R 0RL, England
Penguin Ireland, 25 St. Stephen's Green, Dublin 2, Ireland
(a division of Penguin Books Ltd)
Penguin Books Australia Ltd, 250 Camberwell Road, Camberwell,
Victoria 3124, Australia (a division of Pearson Australia Group Pty Ltd)
Penguin Books India Pvt Ltd, 11 Community Centre, Panchsheel Park,
New Delhi–110 017, India
Penguin Group (NZ), Cnr Airborne and Rosedale Roads, Albany,
Auckland 1310, New Zealand (a division of Pearson New Zealand Ltd)
Penguin Books (South Africa) (Pty) Ltd, 24 Sturdee Avenue,
Rosebank, Johannesburg 2196, South Africa

Penguin Books Ltd, Registered Offices: 80 Strand, London WC2R 0RL, England

First published in 2006 by Sentinel, a member of Penguin Group (USA) Inc.

10 9 8 7 6 5 4 3 2 1

LIBRARY OF CONGRESS CATALOGING-IN-PUBLICATION DATA
Thompson, Keith, 1954–
    Leaving the left : moments in the news that made me ashamed to be a liberal / Keith
Thompson.
      p.   cm.
    Includes index.
    ISBN 1-59523-026-2
    1. Liberalism—United States.   2. Press and politics—United States.   I. Title.
JC574.2.U6T56 2006
320.51'30973—dc22   2006045806

Printed in the United States of America

This is for my mother and my son.

PREFACE

"Man, you sold out big time. . . ."

Of the countless indignant responses I received from liberal readers, this e-mail from Madison, Wisconsin, was my favorite. "Progressives" incensed at my 2005 *San Francisco Chronicle* essay bearing the same title as this book immediately questioned my motives for declaring independence from lockstep liberalism, after President Bush and the U.S. military brought an end to Saddam Hussein's regime.

"So how much did Rove pay you to come over to the dark side? Did they give you a membership in the Bohemian Club? Maybe now you can go skiing with Condi and take beach trips with the Cheneys," wrote an antagonist from Berkeley.

Other than the image of the vice president in beach attire, nothing about the indictments disturbed or even surprised me. Left-wingers believe people are the sum total of their external influences. Since I had changed political stands, green must have changed hands. The money made me do it.

Oh, how those thoughts reminded me of my own. Not anymore. Something happened. I stopped believing all that.

More precisely, over time I lost my faith in the idea that material forces play such an all-powerful role in determining the overall course of a human life. This is not to say objective life circumstances matter only a little; human freedom is very often crippled when a person falls into extreme poverty. What I'm saying is that the power of human consciousness and creativity to surpass and transform life experience matters *a lot*—and in ways that consistently escape the grievance-oriented, victim-based purview of the left.

"Lighten up, guy. Your essay made some fair points, but the best response to the loony left is laughter."

I got that response a lot as well; point well taken. In fact, it's fair to say that the first glimmers of my growing estrangement from the left's pervasive hypocrisy came as moments of amusement.

How hard not to snicker at Jesse Jackson, spending his days flying around the nation in private jets, shamelessly raiding corporate America in the name of the poor while enriching himself and his cohorts—all the while declaring with the straightest of faces: "I may be well dressed . . . but I am still o-*ppressed*."

And Gloria Steinem. After years of declaring romance to be a male-generated myth meant to oppress women, what a festive sight: America's prettiest feminist dating not just males but extremely rich ones, eventually finding herself a multimillionaire to wed, after decades of condemning marriage as the worst patriarchal prison and categorically declaring, "Never." Maybe a fish doesn't need a bicycle, but . . .

But my all-time favorite is Arianna Huffington: always good for a wink, a nudge, or a full belly laugh—especially her cross-country travels in a private jet to warn America away from gas-guzzling SUVs. Now, Arianna may lack the dramatic range of either Zsa Zsa or Eva, but her political pronouncements easily surpass the comic skills of both Gabor sisters—combined. The hair, the husbands, the whole nine yards.

But this book, like the essay that inspired it, did not come about because I think contemporary liberalism is only a joke. My departure from the central premise of America's cultural

left—individuals are helpless pawns of greedy, oppressive, patriarchal forces—took shape incrementally over more than two decades. The decisive swing was less political than philosophical.
My political perspective changed because my views about human
nature and what constitutes "the good society" had changed in
basic ways.

In 2005 I walked away because I'd had my fill of politically
correct rules and taboos: multiculturalism that tries not to offend
anyone and thus must pretend not to notice any differences or
distinctions among people or cultures; moral equivalence that
blames America for everything that goes wrong in the world
while refusing to be judgmental toward the most despicable ty-
rants and despots.

The turning point that led me to write my essay, "Leaving the
Left," was the American left's general refusal to celebrate the stu-
pendous fact that millions of Iraqi voters had risked life and limb
on January 30, 2005, to ratify their own political freedom and
stand up against fascist tyranny. Leading American liberals and
antiwar activists seemed strained to get beyond vague affirmations of Iraq's electoral "accomplishment." Representative Nancy
Pelosi used this underwhelming word repeatedly in remarks that
carried all the enthusiasm of a wake. If this was a funeral, who or
what had died? In the weeks that followed I knew the time had
come to give voice to my steadily growing recognition that the
cultural left had lost its bearings on a whole range of political,
social, and cultural concerns.

"So I guess this makes you a *conservative* now," a Cambridge
reader declared, at once spitting and choking on that italicized
word. I had to admit: the possibility both surprised and intrigued
me. Raised in a town where talk radio callers declared smug satisfaction when Martin Luther King, Jr., was gunned down ("He
had it coming"), I think it's fair to say the word *conservative*
didn't occupy a place of high status in my mind.

Still, having voted for every Democratic presidential nominee since McGovern, I was surprised at the visceral ease with which I checked "independent" when registering to vote after an address change. This was around the time people I admired were saying that lying under oath was okay for a Democratic president so long as the subject was sex and the Republican prosecutor hounding him had ties to (oh, the horror) Big Tobacco. The left's special pleading on behalf of their boy Bill was a moment of truth for me, along with the other turning points I describe in *Leaving the Left*.

I can still recall the original kick of identifying with progressive rhetoric—diversity, compassion, inclusion, tolerance, fairness, equality. How the mere recitation of these secular-god terms reinforced my sense of being part of the vanguard, the leading edge, the inevitable new wave of societal evolution. Yet over time it became clear that the term *progressive* is little more than the political equivalent of a vanity license plate. The progressive banner serves chiefly to give those who fly it license to claim the moral high ground (as against dreaded "regressives" and "reactionaries") while calling for the leveling and redistribution of economic and cultural resources, all the while steering clear of more accurate terms like *Socialist* and *Communist* because of their grim connotations. I never supported those ideologies; just enjoyed the high that came from imagining myself an agent of the larger common good, which I was sure conservatives opposed—plus being sophisticated, urbane, hip, and cool in all the ways that come so naturally to self-championing progressives. But a time came when the ego trip was no longer worth the facade.

In recent years I have come to appreciate the degree to which not only my political views but my overall life perspective had changed as a result of stepping out of the political arena for a considerable period and exploring three life venues that, at first glance, aren't obviously related: journalism, athletics, and parenting.

As an independent journalist I started writing feature stories that drew from sources including developmental psychology, science, comparative religion, social invention, and cultural creativity. I found myself hanging out with parents who chose to home school their kids rather than conform to the dictates of the public-education monopoly; crime victims who view restitution as the missing ingredient in our criminal justice system; divorced dads seeking legal recognition of their crucial role in their kids' lives; and seekers who turn to meditation and other experiential practices to deepen their sense of lived spirituality. Slowly, my previous faith eroded in centralized, bureaucratic service-providing institutions that labor mightily to keep people focused on the bad hands they had been dealt by life and the evil Power Structure that keeps them "oppressed." Their purpose is to ensure people's dependence on the self-congratulatory beneficence ("Oh, we are so *good*") of the liberal elites that comprise those institutions.

Meanwhile, my lifelong passion for physical adventure led me to train for and complete several marathons, trek mountains, and gain more than passing familiarity with the inside of a gym. I can report that not a single coach or trainer ever encouraged me to begin a training program with affirmations cataloging all the ways I might fail. Olympic champions and weekend warriors alike realize that passion, hard work, persistence, and passion for the game are crucial to meeting great challenges on land, air, and water (or just for staying in decent shape). I can still hear the voice of an Austrian-born weightlifter I interviewed for a 1984 *Esquire* story about the crucial importance of mental clarity, focus, concentration, and aspiration. "A single repetition of a bench press with your mind fully present is worth ten repetitions with your mind drifting into space," Arnold Schwarzenegger told me.

Today it's clear to me that human intentionality is critical to success in life domains that far surpass the gym, especially in parenting. Ultimately I write this for my son and his generation. They ask for our best. We cannot let them down.

Whether composing articles about compelling people and works, running on trails overlooking amazing vistas, or feeling that inexpressible upwelling of joy and responsibility when my kid bounds out of his classroom door, I believe our species possesses reservoirs of untapped personal and collective creativity. The idea that the endless proliferation of government is the appropriate measure of human achievement is just no longer credible. It is time for a wiser course, one that starts with the recognition that "some assembly required" applies not just to out-of-the-box bikes and bookshelves but to the shaping of excellence in the lives of individuals and communities.

Back in college, on the Monday before an election day, my political science professor remarked that the word *idiot* comes from the ancient Greek for those who concentrate solely on their own affairs and take no part in community life. Choosing not to vote tomorrow, he said, was a decision to join the idiots. People who made that choice couldn't consider themselves citizens in any meaningful sense. Was that what we wanted?

Thinking back to his stark question, I understood that my silence in the face of what I had learned about the left's true nature verged on idiocy. The liberalism I had embraced during my twenties stood for the freedom and autonomy of the individual, whose liberties were to be guarded over and preserved, and from whom a commitment to personal responsibility was expected. By contrast, the liberalism of the contemporary left finds primary value in the collective, in expanding the scope of a coercive central government, and in defining empowerment in ways that are hard to distinguish from enfeeblement.

It wasn't hard to say good-bye to the collectivist version because I had never truly believed its claims about human nature or the proper way to organize society. Watching the Iraqi election returns, I realized that there was nothing amazing about the left's nonchalant dismissal of freedom and self-determination for the people of Iraq. It was way too late for astonishment—it was time to act. I picked up a pen and began putting words to years of stored images that had been waiting for a voice. I wrote an essay and didn't stop. The result is this book.

CONTENTS

INTRODUCTION

Nightfall, January 30, 2005. Eight million Iraqi voters have finished risking their lives to endorse freedom and defy fascism. Three things happen in rapid succession. The right cheers. The left demurs. I walk away from a long-term intimate relationship. I'm separating not from a person but a cause: the political philosophy that for more than three decades has shaped my character and consciousness, my sense of self and community, even my sense of cosmos.

I'm leaving the left—or more precisely, the American cultural left and what it has become during our time together.

I choose this day for my departure because I can no longer abide the simpering voices of self-styled progressives—people who once championed solidarity with oppressed populations everywhere—reciting all the ways Iraq's democratic experiment might yet implode.

My estrangement didn't happen overnight. Out of the corner of my eye I had watched what was coming for more than three decades, yet refused to truly see. Now it's all too obvious. Leading voices in America's "peace" movement are actually cheering against self-determination for a long-suffering Third World country because they hate George W. Bush more than they love freedom.

Though my first conscious sense of political affinity came in response to Robert F. Kennedy's call to "seek a newer world" and Martin Luther King, Jr.'s poignant hope that his four children would "one day live in a nation where they will not be judged by the color of their skin but by the content of their character," actually I came of age politically in the 1970s, that curiously schizophrenic cultural zone between the revolutionary sixties and the Reagan eighties.

The seventies was a great time to be a liberal. We could claim credit for ending a war and keeping the heat on Richard Nixon until he left the White House in disgrace. The first Earth Day in 1970 put environmental protection on the political map and gave moral ownership of the issue to caring, compassionate progressives. Mary Tyler Moore was busy self-actualizing as a commonsense feminist named Mary Richards; Archie Bunker made it easy to lampoon conservatives as charming bigots; and Gerald Ford's defeat of Ronald Reagan in the 1976 primaries indicated a moderate future for the Republican Party. These cultural and political markers made it easy for me (and others who formed their political identities during this period) to ignore the left's growing incoherence.

To face it directly posed the danger that I would have to describe it accurately, first to myself, and then to others. That could only give aid and comfort to Jerry Falwell, Pat Robertson, and all the other usual suspects the left so regularly employs to keep from seeing its own reflection in the mirror.

On this day I find myself in a swirling metamorphosis. Think Kafka, without the bug. Think Kuhnian paradigm shift, without the buzz. Every anomaly that didn't fit my perceptual set is suddenly back, all the more glaring for being so long ignored. The insistent inner voice I had learned to suppress now has my rapt attention. "Something strange—something approaching pathological—something entirely of its own making—has the left in its grip," the voice whispers. "How did this happen?" The Iraqi election is my tipping point. The time has come to walk in a different direction—just as I had many years before.

I grew up in a northwest Ohio town where conservative was a polite term for reactionary. When Martin Luther King, Jr., spoke of Mississippi "sweltering in the heat of oppression," he could have been describing my community, where blacks knew to keep their heads down, and animosity toward Catholics and Jews was unapologetic. Liberal and conservative, like left and right, wouldn't be part of my lexicon for a while, but when King proclaimed, "I have a dream," I instinctively cast my lot with those I later found out were liberals (then synonymous with "the left" and "progressives").

The people on the other side were dedicated to preserving my hometown's backward-looking status quo. This was all that my ten-year-old psyche needed to know. The knowledge carried me for a long time. Mythologies are helpful that way.

But I also knew there was a world larger than my provincial birthplace. That world poured into my family's living room several times each week, thanks to Walter Cronkite and his far-flung band of correspondents, who delivered news of people standing up for free speech in Berkeley and sitting in for voting rights at Alabama lunch counters; these were stories of marginalized people seeking to shape their own destinies and creating the future in the present moment. I had only one question. How could I get a pass to all this?

For a school assignment about "making a difference in the world," I chose Robert Kennedy's now famous speech to the young people of South Africa. I find this particular passage as exhilarating today as when RFK proclaimed it four decades ago:

"There is," said an Italian philosopher, "nothing more difficult to take in hand, more perilous to conduct, or

more uncertain in its success than to take the lead in the
introduction of a new order of things." Yet this is the
measure of the task of your generation, and the road is
strewn with many dangers. . . . Many of the world's
greatest movements, of thought and action, have flowed
from the work of a single man. A young monk began the
Protestant Reformation, a young general extended an
empire from Macedonia to the borders of the earth,
and a young woman reclaimed the territory of France.
It was a young Italian explorer who discovered the New
World, and the thirty-two-year-old Thomas Jefferson
who proclaimed that all men are created equal. . . .

It is from numberless diverse acts of courage and
belief that human history is shaped. Each time a man
stands up for an ideal, or acts to improve the lot of others, or strikes out against injustice, he sends forth a tiny
ripple of hope, and crossing each other from a million
different centers of energy and daring those ripples
build a current which can sweep down the mightiest
walls of oppression and resistance.

I began my activist career helping to organize voter registra-
tion campaigns in poor neighborhoods. I penned letters to the
editor supporting the Civil Rights Act, defending civil liberties,
citing connections between poverty and crime, arguing for gun
control. I cheered Gene McCarthy's antiwar success in the 1968
New Hampshire primary, though Bobby Kennedy won my alle-
giance when he jumped into the race. I marched with many thousands of Americans in the Washington, D.C., Moratorium against
American involvement in Vietnam, making my way to the stage
in time to hear Richie Havens belt out "Here Comes the Sun."

I held memberships in the ACLU and the NAACP, marched
for farm worker justice, lobbied for women's right to choose and

environmental protections, subscribed to *Ramparts* and the *New York Review of Books,* signed up with George McGovern in 1972, and got elected as the youngest delegate ever to a Democratic national convention. I joined liberal Democrat Howard Metzenbaum's U.S. Senate staff after working as his campaign scheduler and frequent "body guy" (traveling assistant). All my commitments centered on a belief in equal opportunity, due process, respect for the dignity of the individual, and solidarity with people in trouble. To my mind, the early-twentieth-century Americans who joined the resistance to Franco's fascist nightmare had captured the progressive spirit at its finest. I envisioned running for office someday—probably starting with a U.S. House seat, aiming eventually for the Senate.

In short, I was a card-carrying liberal, although I never actually got a card (bookkeeping has never been the left's strong suit). Even without the ID I probably would have continued on the political fast track, except for an unexpected hitch. I burned out. Not yet thirty, I was ready for an alternative to the all-consuming confines of cause-driven protest and the addictive enthusiasm of political campaigns. So I pulled up stakes and headed to northern California to become a freelance journalist. Looking through a wider cultural lens, I started reading widely in psychology, philosophy, social sciences, and religious studies.

My mind was filled with curiosity about exciting new vistas. As the phrase goes, I never looked back. Yet I continued tracking views and events on the left, though with a growing intuition that I was no longer doing so exactly *from* the left.

A turning point came in the 1980s when I wondered why seemingly every Third World political figure pretentiously clad in camouflage and mouthing clichés against the accumulated evils of the West automatically qualified for the sympathies of America's left.

It was hard to grasp the appeal that Daniel Ortega's Sandinista reign of terror held for so many members of Congress and Hollywood activists. What exactly was progressive about Sandinista thugs blowing up churches, torturing pastors, closing down TV and radio stations, and imprisoning labor leaders? When Tom Harkin, Susan Sontag, Pete Seeger, and Noam Chomsky flew to Managua to hold court with Ortega, how come they didn't also make time to interview any of the tens of thousands of Nicaraguans who had fled to Costa Rica, Honduras, and the United States?

A second moment of truth came at a dinner party on the day Ronald Reagan famously described the Soviet Union as the preeminent source of evil in the modern world. The general tenor of the evening was that Reagan's use of the word *evil* had moved the world closer to annihilation. There was a palpable sense that we might not make it to dessert.

When I casually offered that the surviving relatives of the more than twenty million people murdered on orders of Joseph Stalin might not find evil too strong a word, the room took on a collective bemused smile of the sort you might expect if someone had casually mentioned taking up child molestation for sport.

My progressive companions had a point. It was rude to bring a word like *gulag* to the dinner table.

I look back on those experiences as the beginning of my departure from a left already well on its way to losing its grip. Two decades later I watched with astonishment as leading left intellectuals launched a telethonlike body count of civilian deaths caused by American soldiers in Afghanistan. Their premise was straightforward, almost giddily so: When the number of civilian Afghani deaths surpassed the carnage of September 11, the war would be unjust, irrespective of other considerations.

Stated simply: The force wielded by democracies in self-defense was declared morally equivalent to the nihilistic aggression perpetuated by Muslim fanatics.

Susan Sontag cleared her throat for the "courage" of the al Qaeda pilots. Norman Mailer pronounced the dead of September 11 comparable to automobile statistics. The events of that day were likely premeditated by the White House, Gore Vidal insinuated. Noam Chomsky insisted that al Qaeda at its most atrocious generated no terror greater than American foreign policy on a mediocre day.

All of this came back to me as I watched the left's anemic, smirking response to Iraq's election in January. Didn't many of these same people stand up in the sixties for self-rule for oppressed people and against fascism in any guise? Yes, and to their lasting credit. But many had since made clear that they had also changed their minds about the virtues of King's call for equality of opportunity.

These days the postmodern left demands that government and private institutions guarantee equality of *outcomes*. Any racial or gender "disparities" must be considered evidence of blameworthy bias, regardless of factors such as personal motivation, training, and skill. This goal is neither liberal nor progressive, but it is what the left has chosen. In a very real sense it may be the last card held by a movement increasingly ensnared in resentful questing for group-specific rights and the subordination of citizenship to group identity. There's a word for this: pathetic.

I smile when worried friends tell me I've "moved right." I laugh out loud at what now passes for progressive on the main lines of the cultural left.

In the name of diversity, the University of Arizona has forbidden discrimination based on "individual style." The University of Connecticut has banned "inappropriately directed laughter." Brown University, sensing unacceptable gray areas, warns that harassment "may be intentional or unintentional and still constitute harassment." (Yes, *subconscious* harassment. We're watching your thoughts. . . .)

Wait, it gets better. When actor Bill Cosby called on black parents to explain to their kids why they are not likely to get into medical school speaking English like "Why you ain't" and "Where you is," the self-styled "hip-hop intellectual" Michael Eric Dyson, speaking in the name of his blackness, savaged Cosby as a "formerly poor black multimillionaire" whose "lofty goal of proving that blacks are human" amounted to failing "his duties as a racial representative." Translation: Blacks who emphasize universal human themes and become wealthy in the process are race traitors.

When commonsense self-styled pragmatic feminist Camille Paglia mocked young coeds who believe "I should be able to get drunk at a fraternity party and go upstairs to a guy's room without anything happening," Susan Estrich countered that "so long as women are powerless relative to men, viewing 'yes' as a sign of true consent is misguided." Translation: Women who claim to be powerfully self-possessed agents of free will, entitled to exercise the right to choose, cannot be deemed responsible when they make stupid choices that contribute to miserable outcomes.

I'll admit my politics have shifted in recent years, as have America's political landscape and cultural horizon. But who would have guessed that the U.S. senator with one of today's best voting records on human rights would be not Ted Kennedy or Barbara Boxer but Kansas Republican Sam Brownback?

He is also by most measures one of the most conservative senators. Brownback speaks openly about how his horror at the genocide in the Sudan is shaped by his Christian faith, as King did when he insisted on justice for "all of God's children."

My larger point is rather simple. Just as a body needs different medicines at different times for different reasons, this also holds for the body politic.

In the sixties America correctly focused on bringing down walls that prevented equal access and due process. It was time to walk the Founders' talk—and we did. With barriers to opportunity no longer written into law, today the body politic is crying for different remedies.

Today America needs healthy, self-actualizing individuals committed to taking responsibility for their lives, developing their personal talents, honing their skills and intellects, and fostering emotional and moral intelligence. At the heart of authentic liberalism lies the recognition, in the words of John Gardner, "that the ever renewing society will be a free society [whose] capacity for renewal depends on the individuals who make it up." A continuously renewing society, Gardner believed, is one that seeks to "foster innovative, versatile, and self-renewing men and women and give them room to breathe."

One aspect of my politics hasn't changed a bit. I became a liberal in the first place to break from the repressive group orthodoxies of my reactionary hometown.

After the Iraq election my classical liberal spirit was in full throttle when I bid the cultural left good-bye to escape a new version of that oppressiveness. I departed with new clarity about the brilliance of liberal democracy and the value system it entails; the quest for freedom as an intrinsically human affair; and the dangers of demands for conformity and adherence to any point of view through silence, fear, or coercion.

True, it took a while to see what was right before my eyes. A certain misplaced loyalty kept me from grasping that a view of individuals as morally capable of and responsible for making the principal decisions that shape their lives is decisively at odds with the contemporary left's entrance-level view of people as passive and helpless victims of powerful external forces, hence political wards who require the continuous shepherding of caretaker elites.

Leftists who no longer speak of the duties of citizens, but only of the rights of clients, cannot be expected to grasp the importance (not least to our survival) of fostering in the Mideast the crucial developmental advances that gave rise to our own capacity for pluralism, self-reflection, and equality. A left averse to making common cause with competent, self-determining individuals—people who guide their lives on the basis of received values, every-day moral understandings, traditional wisdom, and plain common sense—is merely a faction—and one that deserves the marginalization it has pursued with such tenacity for so many years.

All of which is why I have come to believe, and gladly join with others who have discovered for themselves, that the single most important thing a genuinely liberal person can do now is walk away from the house the left has built. The renewal of any tradition that deserves the name progressive becomes more likely with each step in a better direction.

CHAPTER ONE

RACISM IN THE NAME OF EQUALITY
The Tragic Legacy of Affirmative Action

In order to treat some persons equally, we must treat them differently.

—Supreme Court Justice Harry Blackmun,
*Regents of the University of California
v. Bakke*, 438 U.S. 265, 407 (1978)

The issue before the Supreme Court in the *Bakke* case was clear-cut: Did the special admissions program of the University of California violate the equal protection clause of the Fourteenth Amendment by accepting and rejecting applicants on the basis of race?

For me this was a no-brainer. It is *clearly* unconstitutional—and repugnant—for public institutions to discriminate against people because of their race. Was this not what America had decided when we collectively came to terms with the abhorrent legacy of Jim Crow laws in the South? Hadn't we sat spellbound watching Martin Luther King, Jr., give voice to his dream that his "four little children will one day live in a nation where they will not be judged by the color of their skin but by the content of their character"?

But in the years following the signing of the 1964 Civil Rights Act and the 1965 Voting Rights Act, America's civil rights establishment began to step away from Dr. King's vision, arguing that discrimination on the basis of color might not be such a bad thing after all, if the purpose of inflicting the new round of discrimination against white Americans was intended to remedy the effects of the earlier round of discrimination against black Americans.

Regents of the University of California v. Bakke was the first Supreme Court decision to directly address affirmative action in education. *Bakke* involved the admissions program of the University of California at Davis's medical school. Student applicants had to have a minimum 2.5 grade point average, and only one in six who met that minimum standard was chosen for an interview. Applicants were given a total admission score that included their overall grade point average, their grade point average for science courses, their graded interview score, and their Medical College Admission Test (MCAT) scores, along with measures of their extracurricular activities and letters of recommendation. In 1973, a perfect score was five hundred points. The score increased to six hundred points the following year.

There was a separate admissions program run by a special admissions committee for minority group applicants where the 2.5 grade point average did not apply. Eight slots were reserved for minority candidates; at the time the medical class size was fifty.

Alan Bakke, a white male, applied to the medical school in 1973. His combined score was 468 out of 500. He was denied admission because it was late in the year and the admissions program had ruled that any applicants who scored below 470 would be refused. When he applied again the following year, his application was early, and he achieved a combined score of 549 out of 600. He was placed on the waiting list but eventually was rejected. In both years candidates with lower grade point averages, lower MCAT scores, and lower total combined scores than Bakke's were admitted under the special admissions process.

Did the special admissions program violate the equal protection clause of the Fourteenth Amendment? That was the issue before the Supreme Court in *Bakke*. The Fourteenth Amendment categorically prohibits all state discrimination based on race. The Court had previously held that the Fourteenth Amendment protects Austrian, Chinese, Japanese, and Mexican Americans and Irish resident aliens. It has ruled that "Congress was intent upon establishing in the federal law a broader principle than would have been necessary to meet the particular and immediate plight of the newly freed Negro slaves." So what about Alan Bakke? Would the Fourteenth Amendment protect a white male who was denied admission to a state medical school by a racially discriminatory policy?

On June 28, 1978, in a two-part ruling, the Supreme Court ordered Bakke admitted to the University of California at Davis medical school. A five to four majority held that the U.C. set-aside program violated Alan Bakke's rights under Title VI of the 1964 Civil Rights Act. The court ruled that Bakke had, in fact, been the victim of unconstitutional discrimination. Bakke was admitted to the medical school and went on to get his M.D. and pursue a medical career.

But the Supreme Court did not eliminate the concept of affirmative action altogether. The Court ruled that colleges and universities, and by inference employers, may take race and ethnicity into consideration as one of a number of factors when offering admission or employment. The key point was that prospective students or employees could not be denied entrance or employment *only* on account of race.

Didn't this still amount to reverse racism? That was my question to fellow liberal friends. The essence of their replies: Seems like it, but not really. " 'Racism' is a strong word," said one. "You can't tell a people who've been enslaved that they're now free to start a better life—oh, and sorry about the forced confinement and decades of lynching," she added. "America must atone for what was done," said another friend. How long? "As long as it takes to be effective." That response left me speechless. Effective how—by what measure? "Effective in achieving a color-blind society." Who will decide when the time has come to stop? "The courts, the Congress, the president, the American people as a whole, in the long run."

And so the conversation went among a table full of twenty- and thirty-something well-educated white men and women who cared deeply about race in America. I distinctly remember that none of my compatriots was as amazed by my opposition to race-based policies as I was by their endorsement. When I cited King's words on behalf of color-blind policies, I got sympathetic half nods. The high point (or was it the low?) came when one of my adversaries said, "Look, each of us is privileged, we've all gone to good schools, we've had *our* chance. What's it going to hurt white people to take the seats in the back of the bus that Rosa Parks was going to sit in—at least for a while? It's our turn to feel the sting of being stigmatized. That's what atonement is all about."

That summed it up nicely. A few years later Justice Thurgood Marshall, the Court's first black member, cut even closer to the quick: "You guys have been practicing discrimination for years. Now it is our turn."

I was nine years old on the day King pierced America's conscience. In a very real sense, that was the day I became a liberal in fact if not by label. I also became an individual that day, as opposed to merely a person. When I close my eyes I can still feel the heat of the August sun, playing with a schoolmate in his backyard tree fort on a Saturday afternoon. Unexpectedly, my friend's father called us into the house; there was something important on television.

This was a first. Since when did parents think two boys should be inside watching TV rather than playing outside on a summer day?

We spent the next hour in my friend's living room watching a

Montgomery, Alabama, minister speak to a sea of people in Washington. Before he spoke, I knew only that Martin Luther King, Jr., was 1) controversial and 2) black. By the time he had declared, "I have a dream," I understood how those two facts were related. Suddenly it was clear why so many people considered him a very dangerous man.

When King talked about Mississippi "sweltering in the heat of oppression," he could have been describing our northwest Ohio hometown, where the Klan once had rode with impunity and black neighborhoods were still terrorized at night by vigilantes whose ranks sometimes included men who wore police uniforms for their day jobs. My dad especially let his four sons know bigotry was a habit of weak and contemptible minds, but we couldn't deny that racism was very much alive in our town, along with thinly veiled animosity toward Jews and disdain for the Pope.

Prior to that day I knew that being Jewish made my friend and his family different. I didn't understand exactly how, but it seemed unrelated to my being Episcopalian. Their home was a welcoming place of ideas and conversation and high spirits. On that day it was more: a refuge where I didn't have to try to rationalize or refuse the moral force of King's words. Everyone in front of the TV agreed that this man was speaking truth. His decency was obvious, his call for freedom undeniably right. I had never before experienced such an inspired presence.

Walking home that afternoon I was stopped by a thought that seemed to come from far off. For the first time I realized that the thoughts and opinions running through my mind at any given moment were . . . mine. I was responsible for wherever my ideas might lead and whatever choices I might make, in the town of my birth or the world at large. I had come to my friend's house as a person. When I got back home, I was an individual. The shift was exhilarating, and not a little scary.

———

I am keenly aware that many proponents of racial preferences and color-conscious public policy, reading these words, may think this would be a good time for me to shut up and move on to some other topic. Being white, and therefore ostensibly a beneficiary of a vast array of privileges that go with being white in America, what right do I think I have to criticize affirmative action? Don't I know that the very term "civil rights" is one and the same with the rights of black people? Can't I simply accept that the only way to achieve Dr. King's dream of true equality is through a system of race-based preferences, lowered academic standards, contract set-asides, and employment quotas?

Third question first: No, I can't accept that, because it contradicts the heart and soul of Dr. King's message, and not incidentally, America's defining vision of equal treatment under the law for all Americans. Second question: again, no. Defining civil rights as synonymous with the rights of black people surely made street sense when Dr. King spoke that day in 1963, but to continue down that intellectual road at this point in our national journey must be seen for what it is: a means to lay in place a culture of unending grievance and collective entitlement. Not a wise itinerary.

The first question requires a two-handed answer. On the one hand, of course I have a right to criticize affirmative action. I do so as a citizen of a nation that guarantees me the right to speak on any subject I choose. But of course I realize "what right do you have?" is not intended as a constitutional inquiry. Proponents of racial preferences demand to know what allows someone who checks "Caucasian" on census forms to believe he has a *moral* right to criticize affirmative action without being labeled a racist.

Oh, there was a time when I wrestled hard with those questions. When Justice Blackmun declared that getting beyond the old regime of state-sanctioned racial discrimination would require a new regime of state-sanctioned racial discrimination, in the best spirit of Method acting I made an effort to convince myself that this shift from Dr. King's commitment to equal opportunity for individuals toward enforced equal outcomes for groups was a shift of degree, not of kind. I rationalized: *Affirmative action proponents mean well... Yes, quotas do discriminate on the basis of color and patronize their intended beneficiaries, but they're really just a way to temporarily balance the historic scales.... The policy implications are disturbing, but let's not get into all that because, well, racial preferences are—you know—well intentioned.*

It has taken time and considerable soul searching to pinpoint a hidden aspect of my willingness to suppress my misgivings. I stayed quiet because viscerally I knew that to speak up against the anti-American logic of racial and gender preferences would render me vulnerable to charges of covert racism and sexism. Is this the same as saying I was a classic guilty white liberal? At the time I would have said no, because I enthusiastically believed in the core premise of equality at the heart of both the early civil rights and feminist movements. Today I would say guilt isn't the right word, but it's close. I have come to realize that the civil rights movement invoked a certain kind of shame related to my sense of America's accountability for past injustice.

This is true, I believe, for many white Americans of good will, chiefly left-leaning types, but not exclusively. We figured out that we were presumed racist by virtue of being white in America. We knew, directly if not quite consciously, that this presumption counted as a fact against us in the post–Jim Crow civil rights era. Many white Americans, so-called progressive and other, learned to stay silent about the culturally toxic ramifications of race-based public policies because we carry a degree of racial shame.

Wounded by the knowledge that Jim Crow was a real and vicious force in our nation's recent history, and aware that our country had not lived up to its founding ideals, we had no idea how our very commitment to equality now made us susceptible to being shamed by former victims whose new sense of empowerment depended precisely upon frequent and forceful repetition of our complicity in America's past racism. Consequently, we pretended not to notice when ole Jim Crow got cosmetic surgery and became a fixture of the civil rights establishment, where a new generation of resentment-driven activists had figured out how to gain power by cornering the market on high-minded moral rhetoric.

Just as Jim Crow once publicly empowered torch-bearing vigilantes dressed in white sheets to instill racial terror in black Americans, today he quietly empowers quota-wielding liberals shod in wingtips as they inculcate racial shame in white Americans. Now, as then, he knows the power of racial shame and is unflinching in using it to advance his cause, which is none other than flouting the principles upon which America was founded and to which America has always returned after straying: individual rather than group rights, a single standard of excellence for all, and advancement by merit.

How in the name of equality did the civil rights movement take this ugly and dangerous turn?

I AM A MAN. This was the simple message of a famous picket sign from the early civil rights movement. The sign identified its holder as an individual human, obviously black, doubtless American, probably a descendant of slaves, who expected nothing more (or less) than what Dr. King had hailed as the promise of the Constitution and the Declaration of Independence: "that all men, yes, black men as well as white men, would be guaranteed the 'unalienable Rights' of 'Life, Liberty and the pursuit of Happiness.'"

The civil rights movement made America aware of a wide and tragic gap between promise and performance in making that guarantee real for black people. It was past time to set things right. Against the backdrop of Jim Crow laws that imposed racial segregation on blacks, the Civil Rights Act of 1964 was signed into law with the goal of creating a color-blind society, based on equality of opportunity.

"I will eat the pages of the civil rights bill," Senator Hubert Humphrey, chief sponsor of the act, told his U.S. Senate colleagues, "if anyone can find in it language which provides that an employer will have to hire on the basis of percentage or quota relating to color." Humphrey was spared acute indigestion; Title VII of the act expressly stated that nothing in the law should be interpreted "to require preferences on the basis of race or sex." The bill provided that blacks would be integrated into society like other immigrant groups that held high expectations of achievement for their individuals, groups that had done remarkably well in America even while suffering prejudice.

The aims of this great freedom movement were achieved because its principles were clearly stated, realistic, compelling, and morally right. The movement's goals were founded in recognized constitutional principles that rested squarely in the tradition of justice, fairness, and individual liberty. A new national consensus declared it wrong to judge Americans on the basis of race. To do so was now against the law.

This was a victory for liberalism in the best and most fundamental sense—but the victory was short-lived. Not because of resurgent white racism (the familiar hyperbolized backlash notoriously warned against by left activists), but because many of the activists who had carried the day for equal opportunity suddenly shifted the rules of the game. Equality of opportunity was no longer enough. Nothing short of equal results would remedy the damage caused by America's legacy of immoral yet legal discrimination. Henceforth, any and all continuing disparities would be considered prima facie evidence of culpable bias, regardless of other factors.

The color line was back as a decisive arbiter of American social progress. In the fighting words of Harvard political theorist John Rawls: "Undeserved inequalities call for redress."

Let's examine Rawls's deceptively precise string of words: undeserved inequalities. By whose definition and criteria are specific inequalities undeserved? Redress means rectify, level out, equalize, set right. Marx had some ideas about how to redress undeserved inequalities. History documents how Lenin, Stalin, Mao, and Castro put those ideas into practice. Who will be in charge of the redressing squad this time around?

Over the next two decades America's newly race-conscious civil rights movement worked to shift America's attention from the wrongness of white racism to a demand that white Americans be made to atone for past injustice. It was our time to sit in the back of the bus.

"Two great, immutable forces have driven America's attitudes, customs, and public policies around race," said early civil rights activist Shelby Steele, author and fellow of the Hoover Institution. "The first has been white racism, and the second has been white guilt. The civil-rights movement was the dividing line between the two." White guilt, Steele wrote in a 2002 *Harper's* magazine essay, amounts to a vacuum of moral authority in matters of race that comes from the mere association of white skin with America's past racism.

White guilt is

> the stigmatization of whites and, more importantly, American institutions with the sin of racism. Under this stigma white individuals and American institutions must perpetually prove a negative—that they are not racist—to gain enough authority to function in matters of race, equality, and opportunity. If they fail to prove the negative, they will be seen as racists.

Political correctness, diversity policies, and multiculturalism are forms of deference that give whites and
institutions a way to prove the negative and win re-
prieve from the racist stigma.

Institutions have a stake in being proactive in this, Steele continued. "They must engineer a demonstrable racial innocence to garner
enough authority for simple legitimacy in the American democracy." Any public or private university that admitted students by
academic merit alone would be spurned as racist if it meant no black
or brown faces on campus. "White guilt has made social engineering for black and brown representation a condition of legitimacy."

The phrase "people of color" began to be used to describe the
ways in which race and ethnicity could be politicized, says Ward
Connerly, a prominent activist in what ironically must now be called
the equality wing of the civil rights movement. "Implicit in this
phrase is the coalescing of minorities into a coalition or political
caucus, which, together with white women, constitutes a power
base of sufficient magnitude to preserve race- and gender-based
preferences and to achieve other political benefits for the coalition."

Crucial to the caucus: an orchestrated effort to play upon America's guilt for historic discrimination. For the civil rights activists
and feminist leaders who now demanded equal outcomes for entire
demographic groups, the job was to keep white America and male
America on the hook for past inequality. As these themes took
hold, many self-styled liberals who had earlier championed equal
opportunity began voicing alarm about the implications of this
shift.

Writing in *Public Interest* in 1985, sociologist James Q. Wilson
emphasized the importance of "seeking to induce persons to act
virtuously, whether as schoolchildren, applicants for public assistance, would-be lawbreakers, or voters and public officials." Removing external barriers to full participation was indispensable,

Wilson said, yet the same must be considered true of less readily quantifiable factors such as culture and ethos, character and morality, family background and peer group.

Other liberals of the day joined Wilson's call for a decisive emphasis on a spirit of individual excellence to match the nation's commitment to institutional equality. But the new champions of guaranteed outcomes were not in a listening mood. Indeed, calls for personal and family accountability were just a new way, they said, to "blame the victim." This would become the cultural left's standard response whenever individual responsibility was mentioned as a factor in achieving desired outcomes for minorities and women.

The chasm between classic liberalism and an increasingly hard-edged ideological left has grown rapidly. Obscured in the debate are the differing assumptions of two fundamentally different worldviews.

The phrase "two kinds of people" goes to the heart of how I have come to think about affirmative action. Though I once subscribed to the conventional view of left and right as essentially political terms, about a decade ago it began to seem that these categories more accurately stand for two opposing views of human nature. Today I believe left and right actually represent fundamentally different ways of being in the world, each elemental and self-sustaining in an almost metaphysical sense.

I realize that this is a large claim; extraordinary assertions demand extraordinary evidence. In that spirit, let's go back to a time before the New Deal, the Civil War, and America's founding; an era prior to the Renaissance of the sixteenth century, even earlier than the remarkable cave drawings at Lascaux. Let's think big. Suppose we return to the singular moment, fifteen billion years ago, when the universe itself flared into being.

Blazing with primordial energy never again to be equaled, the cosmos billowed out in every direction, causing the elementary particles to stabilize. Yet this stunning instant was neither an event in time nor a position in space, for the realm or power or source that brings existence is the very matrix out of which the conditions necessary for existence arise in the first place.

You may choose to call that source God. Or perhaps there's a deep self-organizing impulse at the very heart of existence. Or maybe the cosmos is fundamentally random, it just is, it simply happens, don't ask. Philosopher Ken Wilber calls this "the philosophy of 'oops.'" But that's another story.

After a billion years of uninterrupted light the galaxies are born, including our own Milky Way. A supernova explosion creates our stellar system and most of the atoms in our body. Four million years ago an amazing breakthrough takes place. A species called human stands up on just two limbs—on their own two feet, as it were. These became known as Self-Directing Creatives. Other humans, Circumstance-Blaming Reactives, wait to be lifted.

The Creatives look around and say, "What a remarkable place—how can I participate?" Surveying the same vista, the Reactives declare, "This looks rigged, who can I sue?" (Of course I exaggerate; lawsuits are still a ways off. The Reactives' actual first words are more generic: "Who's to blame here?" Followed quickly by: "Not me.")

These strikingly different responses to the primary conditions of existence go to the seemingly metaphysical underpinnings of two very different worldviews. In one sense the two stances can be described as ideal types. Even so, empirically competent observers must admit that the two types keep manifesting, recognizably, in the real world of time and space, mammal department, human subsection.

Creatives tend to see the world as a place teeming with freedom and opportunity, conditions best advanced by individual initiative and most impeded by governmental action. Reactives, by contrast, typically see a world made up of undeserved inequalities to be remedied, ideally through private service-providing elites and government agencies acting in concert. After a few million years it became clear that the Creatives and the Reactives had reached strikingly different conclusions about the primary causes of progress, success, happiness, and suffering. These conclusions are still widely held today.

Let's recap. Creatives generally believe that what's inside people holds the key, while Reactives typically insist exterior factors matter far more. This is to say that Creatives generally underscore subjective factors like work ethic, character and creativity, personal responsibility and moral development. By and large Creatives suspect that the "philosophy of 'oops'" doesn't fully explain the origin and continuing existence of the cosmos, not to mention why taxes more often get raised than lowered. So it's no surprise that when it comes to social interventions to reduce suffering and advance happiness, the typical Creative stands up (no pun intended) for equal opportunity for individuals, guided by the premise that every person deserves a fair shot based upon their potential, heart, and merit. (Reactives once believed this too—as recently as when they opposed the Jim Crow regime of the Deep South.)

Meanwhile, Reactives characteristically point to objective factors: economic conditions, social institutions, environment, and material development—all in the context of a powerful mantra, "history." They regularly invoke this word to ensure that the offspring of formerly oppressed persons are entitled to declare themselves historically oppressed in present time, even when previous objectively oppressive conditions have become history in the conventional (past tense) sense of the word. Accordingly, preferred Reactive social interventions invariably aim to guarantee equal outcomes for entire demographic groups—with race, ethnicity, and gender at the top of the list.

Of course, sometimes there do exist objective, real-world factors that impede equal opportunity. In the world of Jim Crow black people held the status of second-class citizens not because they were shiftless but because a system of brute force kept in place a two-tiered legal structure: one set of rules for whites, a different set of rules for blacks. When Rosa Parks sat down in the front of the bus that famous day and refused to budge, her act of conscious defiance set in motion a wave that helped sweep down Jim Crow's mighty wall of oppression.

Parks's action reflected a prior inner shift, a powerful moment of consciousness that opened up a new interior horizon for her as an individual black woman—a horizon no doubt similar to the mindset of the black man who held aloft this sign: I AM A MAN. Both moments reflect the enduring majesty of the classic liberal vision that emerged out of European Enlightenment ideals, and that eventually gave birth to the freedom quest of the American Revolution. This stands in sharp contrast to the contemporary liberal left's intellectual and moral debt to the French Revolution, a social upheaval that followed a distinctly different course from our own.

Only by understanding the radically different legacies of the two revolutions does it become clear how their fundamentally opposed assumptions, especially about the nature of equality, remain at the heart of major disagreements between liberals and conservatives today. Let's zero in on the two revolutions, starting with the American one.

In 1776 the U.S. Declaration of Independence proclaimed, "We hold these truths to be self-evident, that all men are created equal." Eleven years later in Philadelphia, the core principles of the American Revolution became central to an enduring constitution to provide for a national government based on the rule of law, federalism, separation of powers, and individual rights. In 1789 France's Declaration of the Rights of Man proclaimed, "Men are born and remain free and equal in rights," and this became the defining vision of the French Revolution. Yet five years later, leading revolutionaries assumed dictatorial power in a brutal reign of terror that caused the deaths of up to forty thousand people, all in the name of the principles of that declaration.

How did two revolutions that began with such similar founding ideals come to such different ends? What factors allowed the American Revolution to bring forth a relatively free economy and limited government, while the French Revolution brought forth first anarchy, then dictatorship? The answer is that the two revolutions rested on profoundly different assumptions about the proper stance of human beings toward the given world. This turns out to be a *really big difference.*

The architects of the American Revolution believed all human beings possess a free will, along with reason to direct it. They were convinced that unlimited government corrupts its citizens and undermines the virtues necessary to support a republican form of government, virtues including self-reliance and self-restraint. "There is no truth more thoroughly established," said George Washington, in his first inaugural address, "than that there exists in the economy and course of nature, an indissoluble union between virtue and happiness." For the framers of the Constitution, the pursuit of happiness and the pursuit of virtue were identical. They considered it axiomatic that only a moral people can be a happy people.

By contrast, the architects of the French Revolution subscribed to Jean-Jacques Rousseau's belief that human nature is intrinsically good, but when human beings leave solitary circumstances they are corrupted by society. Reason, rather than being an innate human capacity, somehow simply emerged as a reflection of environmental and cultural forces when humans first entered society, Rousseau insisted. All human language and human thought—moral, political, and religious—are merely the shifting and aimless effects of shifting and aimless external causes.

In Rousseau's world, how are humans supposed to get along with one another? Simple: by abandoning their misguided claims of natural right (including the right to private property) in the name of a social contract based on the good of all. Rousseau put the matter clearly: "People should submit their will to the general will which cannot be wrong and whoever refused would be subject to compulsion, so to express the general will is to express every man's common will." Consider his own account of early human origins: "The first man, who after enclosing a piece of ground, took it into his head to say, *this is mine,* and found people simple enough to believe him, was the real founder of civil society." Then Rousseau calls out:

> How many crimes, how many wars, how many murders, how many misfortunes and horrors, would that man have saved the human species, who pulling up the stakes or filling up the ditches should have cried to his fellows: "Beware of listening to this imposter; you are lost, if you forget that the fruits of the earth belong equally to us all, and the earth itself to nobody!"

If these very different perspectives sound familiar, it's because they still drive many of the great debates in our time—including the controversy about the use of state-sponsored discrimination to correct past state-sponsored discrimination. In the ways that matter most, the left chose the wrong revolution. The left said no to Jefferson's experiment with liberty for the individual and embraced Rousseau's ideas of social equality by force. That fundamental commitment still defines the left's embrace of social engineering through race, ethnicity, and gender. Former leftist David Horowitz argues that two centuries of tragic human experience with impossible socialist schemes has changed the onus of Rousseau's question:

> How many crimes, how many wars, how many murders, how many misfortunes and horrors, would the

human species have been spared, had the world not lis-
tened to this radical imposter, when he assailed private
property, the very foundation of liberty, while invoking
the unlimited powers of the state to make men virtuous
and equal?

In his book *The Quest for Cosmic Justice,* Thomas Sowell defines the debate as no less than one between justice and cosmic
justice. A hallmark of justice (as defined by classical liberalism
and by contemporary conservatism) is a commitment to applying
the same rules and standards to everyone. By contrast, contemporary liberalism (and classical socialism) jettisons this principle
and demands compulsory interventions to equalize prospects or
results. The left's true goal is not justice but cosmic justice, understood as the relief of all misfortune, keyword *all.* From Rousseau
to Rawls, the result is a tragically misguided quest for total (therefore inevitably totalitarian) earthly redemption.

But if affirmative action could be shown to foster black improvement, shouldn't that count for something? Alas, the news on
that front is not encouraging. Blacks from families that make one
hundred thousand dollars a year or more perform worse on the
SAT than whites from families that make ten thousand dollars a
year or less. After decades of affirmative action blacks remain the
lowest performing student group in American higher education.
And once they leave college and enter professions, their own children also underperform in relation to their white and Asian
peers.

Amazingly, history may record as the greatest legacy of affirmative action the sense in which it encouraged ever greater numbers of Americans to grab for the brass ring of victim status. As
Jimmy Durante used to say, "*Everybody* wants to get into the
act."

Attempting to capitalize on rules guaranteeing that a certain percentage of work be set aside for members of minority groups, a 640-pound contractor demanded that he be classified as a minority-group bidder on city of Baltimore contracts because of his size—even though he was unable to visit job sites because he kept falling through wooden stairs.

Meanwhile, a Chicago man complained to the Minority Rights Department of the U.S. Attorney's Office that McDonald's violated federal protection laws because their restaurants' seats are not large enough for his unusually large backside. The indignant eater declared:

> I represent a minority group that is just as visible as blacks, Mexicans, Latins, Asians, or women. Your company has taken it upon itself to grossly and improperly discriminate against large people—both tall and heavyset—and we are prepared, if necessary, to bring federal litigation against your company to comply with the Equal Rights in Public Accommodations Provision. . . . I have a 60-inch waist and am 6 feet 5 inches tall. It is absolutely impossible for me to get service in that restaurant because of the type of seating that you have installed. Furthermore, many of the single seats have such small platforms on the seats that it is impossible for the posterior of an overweight individual to sit on that seat.

Chicago Tribune columnist Mike Royko opined that despite the letter writer's articulate effort to equate his status with that of blacks, Latins, Mexicans, Asians, and women, the writer "was not born with a 60-inch waist and an enormous butt. After a certain age, he created himself and his butt. They are his responsibility. And even the most liberal of liberals would have to agree that [the writer's] 60-inch waist and awesome butt should not be the responsibility of the United States of America."

We can laugh, but the line between comedy and tragedy is often painfully thin. Not long ago C-SPAN carried a Harvard debate on racial preferences between conservative reformer Ward Connerly and left-wing law professor Christopher Edley. During the question session a black undergraduate rose from a disdainful cluster of black students to confront Connerly, who had argued that the time for affirmative action was past. "Once standing, this young man smiled unctuously, as if victory were so assured that he must already offer consolation," reports Shelby Steele. "But his own pose seemed to distract him, and soon he was sinking into incoherence. There was impatience in the room, but it was suppressed. Black students play a role in campus debates like this and they are indulged."

As both a black man and a veteran of the civil rights movement, Steele was dumbstruck at the sight of this young Harvard student rallying his full creative and imaginative powers to argue the fundamental frailty of his own people, and doing so decades after the abolition of antiblack racism in college admissions. Even as Connerly calmly pointed to far less discrimination and far more opportunity for blacks, Steele says,

> The young man must not show faith in the power of his people to overcome against any odds; he must show faith in their inability to overcome without help. . . . [He] must find a way, against all the mounting facts, to argue that black Americans simply cannot compete without preferences. If his own forebears seized freedom in a long and arduous struggle for civil rights, he must argue that his own generation is unable to compete on paper-and-pencil standardized tests.

Like all highly polarized debates about the proper focus of public policy, the controversy about group-based preferences is indeed embedded in a larger set of philosophical issues that seldom reach the doorway of the debate or even the threshold of consciousness. Differences about the very nature of human nature are more often than not at the heart of such questions. I cannot settle all such issues here, but I can at least declare myself on, for instance, certain implications of the originating power that brought forth the universe.

I confess I don't find it easy to believe that the individualized consciousness that democracy depends on—and which the cultural left works so hard to stifle with its collectivist war against self-responsibility—simply "emerged" in some happenstance way, as Rousseau imagined. It's just too close to the philosophy of Oops, the banality of which Ken Wilber rightly mocked. Ours is a cosmos that *differentiates*, giving rise to enormous individualized novelty and creativity at every level of existence. One of the most remarkable expressions of that process is consciousness, the emergence of moral mammals called humans: aware of their surroundings and their relationships with others, but also aware of their own awareness, including promptings from the inner voice called conscience and an ineffable connection with the very spirit of life. How amazing is that?

The revolutionaries of 1776 clearly understood the integral relationship between individual consciousness and the nature of democracy, which depends upon free-thinking moral agents with the capacity for the rational and moral renewal of self and society. The fireball that, according to mainstream science, originated the universe gave way to the first generation of stars, and eventually to our ancestors, who stood on two limbs and later used their hands to shape tools. Before long they unleashed the sun's energy stored in sticks, and learned to use fire to advance their projects. In due course that original creative source took the form of a self-governance that depends on the consent of the governed while also providing for the equal protection of each citizen.

How amazing is *that*?

The individuals who risked their lives by signing the Declaration of Independence understood that happiness can never be guaranteed. What matters is the right of individuals to *pursue* happiness. Maintaining a government that places freedom at the center of its concerns and enforces the law only to defend that freedom is what's at stake.

Here is where we find ourselves. The highest court in the land has declared that government-sponsored discrimination does not violate the Fourteenth Amendment to the Constitution, the relevant clause of which reads: "No state shall . . . deny to any person within its jurisdiction the equal protection of the laws." At other times in our history the Court has endorsed slavery, segregation, and internment based on race and ethnicity. On that blazing summer day in 1963, Martin Luther King, Jr., spoke of his dream that America would come to judge its citizens according not to skin color but to character, as "a dream deeply rooted in the American dream." Because the true force of those words is beyond question, I believe the nation he loved and so eloquently called to justice will awaken from its crippling experiment in compulsory corrective inequality. For the sake of our children, may that day come soon.

CHAPTER TWO

THE GREAT CUYAHOGA VALLEY LAND GRAB

When Eminent Domain Gets Out of Control

Evidence has been mounting for years that something is very wrong in the way the Park Service has been taking private property to add to the vast federal land hoard (about one-third of the U.S. land area). . . . The threat has become reality in the Cuyahoga Valley [where] Park Service officials promised to take only 30 homes but actually have condemned 300, converting the area into a strange, seedy landscape of boarded-up, decaying homes, weed-grown farms and tumbledown roadside stands.

—*Wall Street Journal*, May 25, 1982

The calls were pouring into the Senate office at a furious clip. Nothing surprising; impending legislation invariably stirred up feisty public response. But these calls were different. They had nothing to do with any looming U.S. Senate vote. In fact, the issue that prompted the passionate phone traffic wasn't even on my radar screen. The outpouring of rage took everyone in our office by surprise.

"Keith, you need to talk to some of these people yourself," said Karen, a fellow staffer with a sixth sense for running interference between citizens and the government. Her comment got my attention because my duties didn't generally involve constituent casework. My title was administrative aide for Senator Howard Metzenbaum's central Ohio office, located in Columbus. I was the guy in charge, and I had to admit I didn't have a clue why the folks up near Cuyahoga Valley were so ready to take our office by storm.

That changed when I began taking calls.

"The federal government is stealing our land," a caller declared. Another said, "They say they're acting for the good of the people. Well, we're people up here, and what's happening isn't good for us, it isn't good for our community, it's bad for America, and I demand to know how the hell you and your boss are going to help us."

I didn't know it at the time, but I was taking my first steps into the center of a political and moral cyclone that would rob me of certain illusions about what happens to actual people when they get in the path of the single-minded exercise of federal power. In the bargain, I would also be asked to choose between my loyalty to a political mentor and the pleading of my own conscience. Such a deal.

To set the scene, let me establish exactly how I found myself fielding phone calls from voters who sounded ready to "lock and load" and "ride to the sound of the gunfire."

In 1970 Cleveland attorney and businessman Howard Metzenbaum, having earned a fortune building and running airport parking lots, announced his candidacy for the U.S. Senate. Richard Nixon had been president for just over a year. America was mired in a military quagmire in the jungles of southeast Asia; the antiwar movement was in full force. A political unknown, Metzenbaum ran an insurgent campaign that caught the imagination of liberal activists throughout Ohio.

A tenth-grade student at the time, I was one of them. I thrilled to Metzenbaum's "It's time to reorder our national priorities"

THE GREAT CUYAHOGA VALLEY LAND GRAB

message: anti-Vietnam, reduce military spending, defend the environment, stand up for working people against the giant corporations, fairness, equality, justice, compassion, decency, the public good—the core of the progressive agenda that captured the spirit of the just finished but not yet over 1960s.

After finishing dinner on a cold Ohio February evening, I drove to the local fairground to hear Metzenbaum speak to a gathering of union supporters. An articulate, passionate stump speaker, Metzenbaum's silver mane and strong profile made him actually look like a senator. I was hooked.

I waited for the crowd to dissipate after his speech before I made my move, walking up to the tall man with the senatorial hair, extending my hand like a candidate myself, and catching Metzenbaum's eye. I told him my name and said I wanted to work on his campaign, when could I get started, what could I do to help. The man didn't blink, and I caught the hint of a smile.

"How old are you?" Metzenbaum asked. Sixteen, I said. He paused. "You can absolutely work on my campaign, there's a lot of work to do, and I'm glad to welcome you aboard." On the spot he appointed me his county coordinator, and for the next three months my chief extracurricular activity became campaign work: securing office space for a local headquarters, assembling a brigade of students to distribute campaign literature door-to-door, meeting Metzenbaum's plane at small airports throughout northwest Ohio, and driving him to meetings. I learned to write down names Metzenbaum needed to remember, carry his overcoat and not lose it, keep track of business cards, and find out where the candidate could get a carryout sandwich before getting back on his plane.

Metzenbaum won the Democratic primary that spring but lost to the Republican candidate in the general election. Two campaigns later Ohioans sent Metzenbaum to the U.S. Senate. Just out of college, I said yes when my now good friend and mentor asked me to manage his Columbus district office, managing a staff of three.

Within a few months as Senator Metzenbaum's central Ohio representative, I became familiar with a controversy surrounding the Cuyahoga Valley National Recreation Area. In the mid-1970s Congress had authorized the Park Service to acquire private land within the recreation area, directing that government agency to do so in a way that preserved the culture of the communities along with the wildlife. In 1974 Congress established more than thirty thousand acres as the Cuyahoga Valley National Recreation Area, along the banks of the Cuyahoga River (which famously caught fire in 1969 and became a watchword for pollution).

Expanding the size and number of national parks and recreation areas was a major congressional priority in the midseventies. It wasn't difficult to get excited about preserving rolling floodplains, steep valley walls and ravines, lush upland forests, and refuges for a wide range of species. The human species was likewise supposed to be protected as part of a plan to create "a park for all people, for all time," in the phrase of the plan's architects. "All people" is a powerful phrase—one that goes to the heart of the classic socialist assumption that community and collective are synonymous. When most people think of a community, they tend to think of the individuals who comprise it. Who's looking out for us? That's the question I was getting as a young Senate staffer from northern Ohio citizens—actual, individual people, families with community ties extending for generations who believed their rights and interests were being ignored.

I couldn't answer their questions because I didn't know. And, frankly, part of me didn't want to know. A member in good standing of the Sierra Club, I considered myself an ardent environmentalist. So did my boss, Senator Metzenbaum, whose first campaign for the Senate featured a striking photo of a school-age girl wearing a gas mask, with this headline: Is THIS THE FACE OF

THE FUTURE? Parks for all people are a good thing, and some-times the interests of individuals need to give way to that greater good. Why was that so hard for Bob Lindley to understand?

Lindley was born and raised on a farm in the Cuyahoga Valley area. Bob was nine years old when his dad caught his hired man sleeping out in the field instead of working. Young Bob took over for the hired man, and continued farming. So you can imagine Bob's surprise when two employees of the Park Service showed up to say he wasn't a big-time farmer. We're going to classify you as a hobby farmer, the government men told Lindley. Oh, and by the way: We want your property. Bob said he wanted his property too. We're going to buy your property outright, the men replied.

I heard about Lindley after I promised the people who called Metzenbaum's office that I would investigate and get back to them. I discovered that the legislation creating the Cuyahoga Val-ley National Recreation Area had made clear that the people who lived within the preserve had to be considered a resource no less than the birds, trees, flowers, and waterfalls. The Park Service chose to interpret this mandate in a way that seemed, well, rather odd to the people who lived there. Instead of using scenic ease-ments to allow homeowners to keep their houses and become part of the park, thus preserving the community, the Park Service defied the specific intent of Congress by embarking on a program of compulsory acquisition far more extensive than anything Con-gress and the local people had envisioned.

Using what is called a fee title purchase, the Park Service had set about identifying properties to own. By this arrangement landowners would cease to own their homes but could continue to stay in them for up to twenty-five years as a tenant of the gov-ernment. Slowly but surely No TRESPASSING signs began appear-ing on boarded-up houses throughout the valley.

Longtime resident Bill Erdos got a letter saying the feds needed his property, and that an appraiser would be coming out to determine the value of his spread. When he asked who had made that determination and by what criteria, the Park Service replied: Your property is just on the list. Homeowner Burrell Tonkin asked a Park Service bureaucrat what would happen if he refused to sell. "He says we'll send armed men and take it away from you. And that don't worry me a great deal except for Grandma; it would tear her all to pieces if I went away. So I decided to do the best I could do and just get out."

I took a weekend and drove to the small town of Everett, close to ground zero in the land acquisition campaign. The homeowners I met were some of the most conservation-minded people imaginable. Many of the houses had belonged to families for over a century. These were people who had their own dreams, committed to living their lives free of heavy-handed government bureaucracy. The Park Service bureaucracy was forcing homeowners to sell houses and small businesses that could easily have been integrated into the park. Nobody I talked to could figure out the Park Service's master plan.

Leonard Stein-Sapir was first told they wanted to put in a horse trail. When he showed them how a horse trail would be impossible on his land, the Park Service shifted gears and said they wanted to bulldoze Stein-Sapir's house to create more open space. They "wanted to add another couple of acres to the thirty thousand acres they already had. Then they said they wanted to put in some kind of visitor center, because they think it's so nice. They want to take my home and make it a visitor center."

I returned to work the following Monday and called Washington to see what could be done to help these people retain their homes and keep their communities intact. Metzenbaum's top staffer told me that the boss had decided to wait things out, hoping the crisis would dissipate on its own. I countered that by saying, if he intervened on behalf of the local homeowners he could get the best of both worlds: doing the right thing, and getting positive press coverage. When Metzenbaum called me the next day, he wasn't in a merry mood. And everyone who worked for Howard Metzenbaum knew to steer clear of his dark side.

"What the hell are you doing driving up there on weekends, representing me without authorization?" he demanded. Fair point. I had figured that by going on my own time I didn't need Washington's approval. "Think again, chief," he said. ("Chief" was the nickname he used when he liked my stay-late, work-long attitude during the campaign. This time, the moniker didn't suggest he was about to give me a raise.) "Anytime and anywhere you go as a member of my staff, that makes you my representative. I don't like what's happening to some of these homeowners any more than you do. But this is one hell of a national park, and it's good for Ohio and good for America."

Metzenbaum continued, "This thing has become a damned hornet's nest. The property-rights groups have gotten involved, and those bastards spent a lot of money to make sure I never got to the Senate. Well, I'm here, and you're here, too, and we're going to remember who we serve and why. The rights of the few have to give way to the needs of the majority—and besides, the homeowners are getting paid for their land." I'll never forget what came next. "Keith, if you stay in politics and if you ever run for office, you'll learn what's best for the people as a whole never satisfies everybody. Parks require property. You can't make an omelet without breaking eggs. Now stay away from Cuyahoga Valley. Forget about it."

For the rest of my days as a Senate staffer, I stayed away but didn't forget. In retrospect, I was probably already thinking like a journalist when I made my field trip to Everett. Given a choice between develop and conserve, it wasn't a hard choice for me when the issue was framed in general terms. But here the Park Service was the developer, and the property owners inside the newly created park were the actual conservationists.

The turnabout was remarkable, and it created an enormous conflict in my mind. I admired the overall thrust of Metzenbaum's work, yet I couldn't convince myself that what was happening to the homeowners was right or just. Nor was I willing to try. I managed to tamp down the dissonant voices in my head by concluding—not entirely convincingly—that Cuyahoga Valley was an anomaly, an exception to the rule, an administrative agency that had run amok in this one instance. Most of the time park developers are the good guys; most of the time complaining homeowners are selfishly unmotivated by the common good. I slept better.

Meanwhile, the Park Service proceeded to force homeowners to sell their property, in clear violation of the legislation's intent to keep the culture intact through the use of easements. It turned out that the Park Service had no real acquisition plan other than to move as many people out in the name of preservation. The Park Service spent hundreds of thousands of dollars buying homes they didn't need, and then proceeded to bulldoze many of them. They destroyed family homesteads that had been in the same families for generations, for no real reason. Out of 500 houses, over 425 were taken. Communities were destroyed, churches and schools closed, houses boarded up, and the tax base eroded by land acquisition overkill.

Natalie and Bob Valcanoff had run a flower shop for close to three decades. They were told to sell whether they liked it or not. Upon their refusal, the Park Service said that if the Valcanoffs didn't accept their offer they would face condemnation. According to Bob, "Ninety days is not nearly enough time to move a business that's been here for twenty-eight years." Park superintendent Bill Birdsell was unapologetic.

"The flower shop itself is a commercial operation that was incompatible with the park being developed as a public use, so that had to go. The house will eventually be disposed of, as will the flower shop. We will try to find adaptive use of any of the structures we can, if there's an administrative need. But the size of that shop and its present location we don't project any use for that at the present time. It's simply to be obliterated and become public use area along the river there."

"Incompatible . . . disposed of . . . obliterated"—these images call to mind what the legendary American officer had said of a Vietnamese village, that it was "necessary to destroy it in order to save it." If My Lai had been an atrocity, so was Everett.

I resigned from Metzenbaum's staff not because of Cuyahoga Valley but because I was exhausted from politics and had changed my sights to journalism. After moving to the beautiful San Francisco Bay Area, there were moments when I felt like I was in a witness relocation program—I was that glad to be free of the constant turmoil of things political.

My hiatus was shorter than expected. In 1980 Senator Alan Cranston introduced legislation to declare California's central coast a national scenic area. I had become familiar as a hiker and distance runner with the backcountry of Big Sur, and with the effective network of state and local environmental protections that so successfully had created a true ecology of human and natural resources. It's no exaggeration to say that to be a citizen of the majestic Big Sur is to be a conservationist; the categories cannot easily be teased apart. The vast majority of the community was opposed to the Cranston bill, and I didn't have to think twice about joining their ranks. Having seen what happened to Cuyahoga Valley, I determined to do everything I could to help keep Big Sur and the surrounding areas free from those who would protect the area into cultural and bureaucratic oblivion.

So I joined a confederation of central coast citizens to defeat the Cranston bill, and agreed to travel to Washington to lobby senators. Along the way I forged an unexpected alliance with Chuck Cushman, executive director of the American Land Rights

Association, a grassroots group started in 1978 as the National Park Inholders Association. Its mission is to protect landowners from unwanted private property acquisition by the National Park Service. An inholder owns private property or some other equity interest inside or adjacent to a federally managed area. There are thousands of inholders across the United States. Prior to Cuyahoga Valley I would have considered Cushman a hired gunman for greedy developers and selfish property owners, and thus a dangerous guy in the eyes of a culturally sophisticated *New Yorker* reader and regular at leftish wine-and-cheese fund-raisers.

Turns out Cushman found me somewhat confounding as well.

"You worked for *Metzenbaum*?" he asked at our first meeting. Yes, I said. "*Howard* Metzenbaum?" I nodded. Cushman looked at me with a self-mocking incredulity. "How'd you get here?" he asked. His tone suggested that "here" involved a harrowing escape from the gravitational field of the Death Star just in the nick of time.

I smiled at that, but held on to my suspicions. Maybe Chuck Cushman and I were in agreement about wanting to correct damage done in the name of preservation at Cuyahoga Valley, and both wanted to keep the same abuses from befouling the California coast in the name of "all people for all time," but it was a pretty good guess that Chuck Cushman and I weren't natural allies.

I was a liberal. Surely he was a conservative. I favored responsible public use of private lands. He was a private-property rights advocate. I didn't know it at the time, but I found out that Cushman likewise believes in responsible public use of private lands. He loves land and believes in protecting it. He also believes keeping private lands in private hands is generally the best means to achieve that goal. I credit him with introducing me to the multiple-use school of land management, which in name sounds like some high-flown theory but in fact is recreationists, hunters, miners, sportsmen, landowners, ranchers, the handicapped, the elderly, and many others working together throughout the United States to support access to and multiple-use of federal lands, and to oppose selfish single-use designations that limit access for millions of American families.

Chuck and I talked for over an hour at his Washington, D.C., office, not only about Cuyahoga (he knew the situation well, having supported the homeowners' cause) but about dozens of other national parks where inholders are regularly treated like second-class citizens.

A Firesign Theater album title of the midseventies, *Everything You Know Is Wrong,* gives a sense of how topsy-turvy it felt for a backpacking, mountain-trekking, snowshoeing, ridge-running environmentalist like me to suddenly be allied with a guy who worked 24/7 to advance the cause of private property rights. Oil and water? Hardly. Turned out we had a lot in common. Cushman had served the Park Service in the second Student Conservation Corps in Olympic National Park in 1959, and his father had been a Park Service ranger. Chuck had been a volunteer with the Audubon Society at what is now known as Channel Islands National Park. His son worked for the Park Service in the living history center in Yosemite National Park, and Chuck later served as a member of the National Park System Advisory Board.

Meanwhile, the California coalition to defeat the Cranston bill made the rounds to educate members of the Senate Committee on Energy and Natural Resources on the adequacy of Big Sur's present environmental protections and on the dangers of a federal solution for a nonexistent problem. Senator Metzenbaum was a member, and I looked forward to seeing him again for the first time since leaving his staff to take on issues as a journalist rather than to engage them politically. While on his staff I had met with plenty of citizen lobbyists over the years; now I was on the other side. The name of the game: persuading members of Congress on the merits of your cause.

On arriving I spent some time briefing the senator's staff member who handled parks and natural resources. Midway through the conversation, familiar blinking lights indicated a Senate vote was getting under way. "Hope you're wearing track shoes," his secretary said, making clear that my time with her boss would involve forward momentum at a decent pace. Sure enough, Metzenbaum shot out of his private office and whirled me toward the door, and we sped down the hallway. After a few friendly exchanges about my work and our families, we got down to business.

"I understand you're in town to testify against Alan Cranston's coastal protection bill," he said, as we climbed aboard the subway from the Russell Senate Office Building to the Capitol. "Tell me why." I did precisely that, giving him a five-minute overview. He seemed a bit distracted—senators rushing to vote are like that—but when I mentioned Cuyahoga Valley his attention focused. Actually, the phrase seemed to startle him. Metzenbaum said he "regretted what happened to Cuyahoga Valley," then added that he was not inclined to oppose the California legislation because he trusted Alan Cranston's "sense of the situation," or something like that.

I had expected as much, and knew there would be time for hard-core lobbying if and when the bill made it to the Senate floor. We parted company at the doorway to the Senate, with Metzenbaum asking me to give a full briefing to his staffer who handled parks and natural resources. I returned to his office and told the staffer I would be testifying against the Cranston bill the following day. As a courtesy, I wanted Metzenbaum to know I intended to describe in detail what the Park Service had done to Cuyahoga Valley. I would strongly urge the committee members not to allow the same thing to happen to Big Sur.

Let's say it was a tense moment. "I think the senator wouldn't consider that helpful," he said. I nodded, and said my goal was to help California, and I hoped his boss would agree to do the same thing by voting against the Big Sur bill. I left Metzenbaum's office knowing that they thought I was on the wrong side of the issue. I felt a sudden burst of freedom. The following morning I got a call from the staffer; call it the other shoe dropping.

"I spoke with the senator, and he wanted you to know how much he appreciates your passion for this issue, and he expressed his hope that you can find a way to talk about your situation in California without making unwarranted generalizations about Cuyahoga Valley. He asked me to say he would appreciate your respect on this matter." Metzenbaum had taken a lot of heat in the Ohio press for not intervening on behalf of homeowners, if only symbolically.

For reasons I understood at the time and disagreed with at the time, Metzenbaum had made a conscious decision to steer clear of Cuyahoga Valley. I suspect he felt he should have done something for the "little guy" he talked about constantly during his campaigns. He didn't want to be reminded of that. I wouldn't want to be, either.

That afternoon I sat at a long wooden table with several witnesses at a public hearing chaired by Senator Ted Stevens of Alaska, who called on me to close out a long afternoon of heated testimony.

> Mr. Chairman and distinguished senators:
>
> I am here because I love open space and wild terrain. I have hiked through miles of wilderness and I celebrate the great spirit of John Muir as a visionary of the natural world. I hold memberships in the Sierra Club and the Wilderness Society. I am a proud environmentalist who believes in protecting and preserving natural resources. I love the central California coast, especially the wild canyons of Big Sur. For these reasons and

more, it may surprise you to learn that I have come here today to join my voice with those who believe Senator Cranston has proposed the wrong bill for the wrong place at the wrong time.

Witnesses who preceded me have laid out a solid case against the Cranston bill, so I will not take your valuable time by repeating their arguments in the few minutes I have before this committee. Furthermore, I will not have much to say about California's central coast, other than to emphasize that a tapestry of state and county government and private organizations and dedicated citizens currently serves to protect the California coast. Simply stated, no federal solution is required because no federal problem exists.

But if you are looking for an opportunity to create a serious local problem, then a federal solution may be just the thing to consider. And rather than start from scratch, I can tell you just the place to look for a model of how to preserve natural resources in a way that eradicates decades and even generations of wise human stewardship.

That place is the Cuyahoga Valley National Recreation Area in Ohio, the state where I was born and raised and became a political activist. I worked on the campaigns of your colleague Mr. Metzenbaum and served on his Senate staff in his Ohio office. During that time I witnessed a human tragedy that did not need to happen. That same tragedy is poised to happen again and again if the same destructive policies are allowed to remain in place.

In the mid-1970s, the National Park Service set about the making of a national park called the Cuyahoga Valley National Recreation Area. Those who planned the park intended to create a refuge of peace and beauty for all time. The legislation called for preserving culture as well as nature. But that's not what happened.

The local people were assured that only a handful of private residences—fewer than thirty—would need to be acquired on a compulsory basis. In fact, the Park Service embarked on a land acquisition program more comprehensive than anyone expected or even imagined. More than four hundred of the original residences have been acquired in fee already or are in condemnation. The Park Service administrator in charge of the program refused to reveal his master plan. This deprived concerned citizens of their right to know the exact intentions of the Park Service. Cuyahoga Valley could have been a success without much land acquisition.

Incredibly, the Park Service has no use for many of the homes, so they're being torn down or turned over to the fire department to burn for practice. A farmer for more than twenty years, Bob Lindley was categorized as a "hobby farmer" and had his place torn down and hauled away in trucks. Amazingly, then he was contacted and asked if he might like to buy back his old property.

Today the Lindley property is open space. The destruction of the community is nearly absolute—churches closed, library struggling to stay open, the school system divided. "One size fits all" is bad policy for clothing and worse policy for national land preservation. As the psychologist Abraham Maslow said, "If the only tool you have is a hammer, you tend to see every problem as a nail."

If ecology is a good thing, as I believe it is, and if wise ecology depends on diversity and a variety of relationships between human beings and their natural and social environments, does a monolithic approach to park development make ecological sense? Doesn't "multiple use" suggest a more sophisticated ecology? I am a liberal Democrat, but garden-variety intellectual honesty requires me to say no to the first question, and yes to the second.

Mr. Chairman, the Founders of our Republic understood the crucial necessity of private property, the right to which was not to be abridged except under the most exacting and specific conditions. James Madison, in one of the most famous of the *Federalist Papers,* wrote that the right to acquire and protect property to be one of the fundamental, inalienable natural rights of mankind, and it is so recognized in most of the original state constitutions and nearly all of the subsequent state constitutions. Pennsylvania's Constitution of 1776 is fairly typical, recognizing "[t]hat all men are born equally free and independent, and have certain natural, inherent, and inalienable rights, amongst which are, the enjoying and defending life and liberty, acquiring, possessing and protecting property, and pursuing and obtaining happiness and safety."

I love America's national parks, and could happily spend the rest of my life visiting them. I love America's founding traditions even more than her parks, however, and I understand the dedication of those who say they are willing to spend the rest of their lives defending those traditions. As F. A. Hayek writes in *The Road to Serfdom:*

"What our generation has forgotten is that the system of private property is the most important guaranty of freedom, not only for those who own property, but scarcely less for those who do not. It is only because the control of the means of production is divided among many people acting independently that nobody has complete power over us, that we as individuals can decide what to do with ourselves. If all the means of production were vested in a single hand, whether it be nominally that of 'society' as a whole or that of a dictator, whoever exercises this control has complete power over us."

Bearing in mind the lessons of Cuyahoga Valley should motivate the United States Senate to put aside Senator Cranston's ill-advised plan to federalize the central California coast.

The Senate committee never acted—not a problem because America acted first by electing Ronald Reagan president, which ensured that the days of monolithic federal land protection plans were done, but the war against American homeowners is far from won. Under the Supreme Court's 2005 *Kelo v. New London* decision, "all private property is now vulnerable to being taken and transferred to another private owner, so long as it might be upgraded," in the words of dissenting justice Sandra Day O'Connor.

Susette Kelo had long dreamed of owning a home that looked out over the water. In 1997 she purchased and lovingly restored her small pink house in Connecticut, where the Thames River meets the Long Island Sound, and has enjoyed the magnificent view from its windows ever since. Just down the street, the Dery family has lived in Fort Trumbull since 1895; Matt Dery's parents— his next-door neighbors—purchased their house during the McKinley administration. The richness and vitality of their neighborhood mirrors the American dream of home ownership. Thanks to the City of New London, that dream is turning into a nightmare.

In 1998, the pharmaceutical corporation Pfizer constructed a plant next to Fort Trumbull, and the city resolved that someone else could make better use of the land than the people of Fort Trumbull. So the city gave over its power of eminent domain— the ability to take private property for public use—to the New London Development Corporation (NLDC), a private body, to acquire the entire neighborhood for private development. As the Fort Trumbull neighbors discovered, when private entities exert government's awesome power of eminent domain, and can rationalize taking property with the nebulous claim of "economic development," all homeowners are in trouble.

Public response to the 5–4 *Kelo* ruling has been widespread and nearly unanimous in its outrage. Homes and churches, small businesses and open pieces of land can now be taken by the government, only to be handed over to private developers for their private gain. Before *Kelo*—a ruling supported by the Court's most liberal members—government could only take private property for public use, such as for roads, utilities, hospitals, or military bases. Now those limits are gone. Large corporations and developers with deep pockets can join with local governments to come up with all kinds of plans to take away property.

The U.S. Supreme Court may have ruled, but the fight isn't over. *Kelo* left open the door for states to enact laws that specifically restrict the seizing of property in the name of private economic development. A movement to block the ruling's effects is under way in several states to ensure that all small business owners and homeowners can regain their rights to private property.

"Now is the time for Americans to demand their state and local lawmakers protect homes and small businesses from eminent domain for private profit," says Dana Berliner, a senior attorney with the Institute for Justice, a Virginia-based organization that litigates to secure economic liberty, school choice, private property rights, freedom of speech, and other vital individual liberties, and to restore constitutional limits on the power of government. "Rarely does a single issue generate such universal outrage. Americans understand that the U.S. Supreme Court has declared open season on home and small business owners."

Over forty state legislatures have enacted or will soon consider eminent domain reform in the wake of *Kelo*. Texas and Alabama both have enacted laws aimed at preventing exactly what *Kelo* allowed. Ohio established a one-year eminent domain moratorium as it studies the issue. Michigan, whose own state supreme court rejected *Kelo*-style takings in 2004, referred a measure to its voters to affirm their case law. And the U.S. Congress is on the verge of restricting federal economic funds from being used by eminent domain abusers.

"What's been passed so far are good first steps, but they are only first steps, and much more needs to be done if small property owners are to be protected," says Berliner. "Nearly every state needs not only to restrict the use of eminent domain for private commercial development, but also to reform their blight laws to stop bogus blight declarations. Unless both of those reforms are done, and done in the right way, this abuse will continue."

More than a year after the Supreme Court decision, Susette Kelo's house still stands, but her home is a member of an endangered species. The Cuyahoga Valley residents whose homes were condemned and destroyed can't say the same. Big Sur's future is uncertain. The U.S. Forest Service has embarked on a program to acquire as much private land as possible. Rather than overtly asking Congress to federalize the entire area, the Forest Service and other agencies are buying up the private land first, and will ask Congress to designate the area later. Many in Big Sur are distressed at this indirect method of federalizing the area. They call it the "Pac-Man National Park," after the video game that was won by devouring your opponent one bite at a time. Working closely with the Forest Service are various conservation organizations that make millions buying private land and flipping it into government ownership.

"These private groups have learned to make a business out of dismantling rural American communities like Big Sur," says Big Sur local rights activist Michael Caplin, who grows weary of the argument that individuals must step aside for the collective good. "There is no collective," he says. "There are only individuals. Sacrifice individuals for a collective ideal, and you sacrifice the collective, one individual at a time. You can go out and shake the hands of individuals, but you can't shake the hand of the collective. It ain't there. It's a dream. The best way to make the collective ideal come true is to sacrifice no one, treat each individual fairly. Then the dream can come true one person at a time."

CHAPTER THREE

"THIS BEGINS TO LOOK LIKE SICKNESS"

Sad, What Happened to Feminism

I feel that "man-hating" is an honorable and viable political act, that the oppressed have a right to class-hatred against the class that is oppressing them.

—Robin Morgan, *The Demon Lover,* 1989

Am I now, or have I ever been, a feminist sympathizer? Yes, indeed. During my mid-1970s undergraduate years, the core premise of the women's movement made considerable sense: Suppose we agree to extend "all men are created equal" to include women. The females I went to class with and exchanged ideas with and sometimes flirted with were invariably articulate, self-possessed, fiery, keen on pursuing big goals and leading accomplished lives in fields that were once the sole province of males. If they hated guys it was one of the better-kept secrets on campus.

"We ask no better laws than those you have made for yourselves," is how Elizabeth Cady Stanton put it, back in 1854. "We need no other protection than that which your present laws secure to you." That basic idea still resonates for me and, I think, most American men. Surely the vast majority of women share Stanton's vision—which ironically puts them at odds with most of today's self-described feminists.

The heart and soul of contemporary feminism is no longer impelled by mere equality. No, the fundamental goal is to liberate women from the pervasive system of male dominance known as the patriarchy, a sex/gender structure that ensures all men positions of dominance and privilege while relegating women to the status of permanently oppressed victims.

But wait. Public opinion surveys continue to show that the vast majority of women do not see themselves as victims of any such conspiracy. So it stands to reason that any theory of a unique "woman's vantage point," according to radical feminist Alison Jaggar, must be able to "explain why it is itself rejected by the vast majority of women." Here is how Jaggar answers her own question: Women are brainwashed by the patriarchy!

But I'm getting ahead of myself (which may or may not be a guy thing). First things first: Return with me now to the days when equality between women and men mattered more than blaming men for the assorted evils of Western civilization, the days before radical feminists like Robin Morgan, Catharine MacKinnon, and Andrea Dworkin abandoned the project of equality, opting instead to vilify all men as men, with Dworkin going so far as to declare, "Marriage as an institution developed from rape as a practice. Rape, originally defined as abduction, became marriage by capture. Marriage meant the taking was to extend in time, to be not only use of but possession of, or ownership."

We return to Seneca Falls, New York—July 14, 1848. On that day the following announcement appeared in the *Seneca County Courier:* "A convention to discuss the social, civil, and religious condition and rights of women will be held in the Wesleyan Chapel, at Seneca Falls, N.Y., on Wednesday, and Thursday, the 19th and 20th of July current; commencing at 10 o'clock A.M." The unsigned notice was written by four women meeting in the home of Richard Hunt, a well-heeled reformer who had agreed to help them organize the convention. Two of the women, Elizabeth Cady

Stanton and Lucretia Mott, would later gain worldwide renown. The small table on which they drafted the equivalent of a press release is today on exhibit at the Smithsonian as an artifact of the moment when American women started the political struggle to win such basic rights as those to divorce without losing property and children, and to be educated. This cause would go on to include the right to vote and the achievement of full legal equality.

The media response was swift. These were "childless women," "divorced wives," and "sour old maids." The four women had expected as much, and they got used to it. Looking back years later on the women who traveled to Seneca Falls, Elizabeth Cady Stanton and Susan B. Anthony wrote that "they had not in their own experience endured the coarser forms of tyranny resulting from unjust laws, or association with immoral and unscrupulous men, but they had souls large enough to feel the wrongs of others without being scarified in their own flesh."

The convention voted to adopt the Declaration of Sentiments written by Elizabeth Cady Stanton, who had adapted the words of Jefferson's Declaration of Independence but specified that the liberties demanded were for women as well as men. Here is the preamble:

> When, in the course of human events, it becomes necessary for one portion of the family of man to assume among the people of the earth a position different from that which they have hitherto occupied, but one to which the laws of nature and of nature's God entitle them, a decent respect to the opinions of mankind requires that they should declare the causes that impel them to such a course.

And she went on to speak of the truth "we all hold to be self-evident, that all men and women are created equal."

As with Jefferson's famous document, the Seneca Falls orga-
nizers presented a list of grievances, detailing injuries that women
suffer at the hands of men. Among them:

> He has never permitted her to exercise her inalien-
> able right to the elective franchise. . . . He has com-
> pelled her to submit to laws, in the formation of which
> she had no voice . . . thereby leaving her without repre-
> sentation in the halls of legislation. . . . He has made
> her, if married, in the eye of the law, civilly dead . . . in
> the covenant of marriage, she is compelled to promise
> obedience to her husband, he becoming, to all intents
> and purposes, her master—the law giving him power
> to deprive her of her liberty, and to administer chas-
> tisement.

Seneca Falls zeroed in on specific injustices of the type that
social policy could repair by making the laws equitable. The conference was organized by both men and women; the active participation of men was welcomed. The well-defined, tangible,
realistic goals that grew out of Seneca Falls were eventually
achieved because they were clearly grounded in American ideals
such as equality, fairness, personal responsibility, and individual
liberty. Yet with all due respect, it is clear that these women had
no idea just how oppressed they would continue to be after their
remarkable goals had been achieved. To get a sense of the depths
of victimization that remained, let us jump back closer to our
time.

In 1988, Syracuse University professor Kathryn Allen Rabuzzi
wrote a book describing in no uncertain terms the abject horror
that goes with being a woman in a patriarchy where men collectively keep women down. Rabuzzi opens her book by recounting
this event:

As I was walking down a sleazy section of Second Avenue in New York City a few years ago, a voice suddenly intruded on my consciousness: "Hey Mama, spare change?" The words outraged me. . . . Although I had by then been a mother for many years, never till that moment had I seen myself as "Mama" in such an impersonal, external context. In the man's speaking I beheld myself anew. "I" disappeared, as though turned inside out, and "Mama" took my place.

Oh, but the worst was yet to come; Ms. Rabuzzi reveals that the panhandler's term caused in her a "shocking dislocation of self." Even more shocking, this experience was not hers alone—it was shared by other women in isolated corners of the patriarchy. University of Illinois feminist theorist Sandra Lee Bartky recounts:

It is a fine spring day, and with an utter lack of self-consciousness, I am bouncing down the street. Suddenly . . . catcalls and whistles fill the air. These noises are clearly sexual in intent and they are meant for me; they come from across the street. I freeze. As Sartre would say, I have been petrified by the gaze of the Other. My face flushes and my motions become stiff and self-conscious. The body which only a moment before I inhabited with such ease now floods my consciousness. I have been made into an object. . . . Blissfully unaware, breasts bouncing, eyes on the birds in the trees, I could have passed by without having been turned to stone. But I must be *made* to know that I am a "nice piece of ass": I must be made to see myself as they see me. There is an element of compulsion in . . . this being-made-to-be-aware of one's own flesh, like being made to apologize, it is humiliating. . . . What

I describe seems less the spontaneous expression of a
healthy eroticism than a ritual of subjugation.

Now, bear with me for one more account in this compelling
genre of male treachery and female degradation. Author of *The
Beauty Myth,* a book documenting societal pressures on women to
conform to a standard of beauty, Naomi Wolf found herself be-
sieged by critics who mocked her for flipping her long hair around
in photo shoots. What these critics didn't get was that her well-
attended prettiness actually confirmed her thesis that our culture
rewards bombshells who can write well about suffering beauty.
Addressing the Scripps College graduating class of 1992, Wolf described an incident from her own commencement exercises when
she graduated from Yale eight years before. Dick Cavett, the
speaker, had made the experience a "graduation from hell." Cavett,
himself a Yale alumnus, had started his address with an anecdote
about his undergraduate days: "When I was an undergraduate . . .
the women went to Vassar. At Vassar they had nude photographs
taken of the women in gym class to check their posture. One year
the photos were stolen, and turned up for sale in New Haven's red-
light district. . . . The photos found no buyers." According to Wolf,
the moment was overwhelmingly shocking. "There we were, silent
in our black gowns, our tassels, our brand-new shoes. We dared
not break the silence. . . . That afternoon, several hundred men
were confirmed in the power of a powerful institution. But many
of the women felt the shame of the powerless: the choking silence,
the complicity, the helplessness."

These three very personal accounts have something important
in common, namely: Sophisticated researchers have not been able
to turn up evidence that the writers were attempting to be funny
or mischievously trying to put one over on naive readers. These
women are being *serious,* and so is Christina Hoff Sommers when
she asks, "Is it possible that the Yale women were so stricken by

Cavett's tasteless joke? Did the Scripps women really need a survival kit? If these privileged young women are really so fragile, what could Wolf's survival kit do for them anyway?" Sommers continues:

> Earlier in this century, many households still had smelling salts on hand in the event that "delicate" women reacted to displays of male vulgarity by fainting. Today, women of delicacy have a new way to demonstrate their exquisitely fragile sensibilities: by explaining to anyone who will listen how they have been blighted and violated by some male's offensive coarseness.

When I later spoke with a woman who was in the audience for Wolf's graduation speech, I was eager to hear how she had responded. "I have to say I was appalled," she laughed. "I'm a feminist. I've worked with abused women, and I know what goes on. I had this horrible sinking feeling after Naomi Wolf left the stage. I remember thinking, 'So this is what happens to the feminism of Susan B. Anthony? This begins to look like sickness.' "

But could the true sickness belong to a society that is misogynist to its roots? Could it be that women and men are created equal, and the reason females do not have more power is that they have been oppressed by the males for centuries? Or perhaps the sexes are not created equal but are very different, with different values, different wants and drives, and especially different modes; and the most important problem with this world is that male values have dominated the female values. It was not always this way. Humans started out with women-centered societies that honored female values—relational, caring, compassionate, life-affirming values—and then there came a time when, wham, the males stepped in and repressed and oppressed those values.

Ideas like these were more than floating around during my

mid-1970s college years. Given the cloistered, hothouse intellectual atmosphere of the average university campus, the patriarchy
theory of culture easily took hold. I can't say I ever subscribed to
the theory, but I was at least open to the possibility that sex-based
power structures could be at once pervasive and largely invisible,
precisely because they were taken to be the norm. White beneficiaries of the Jim Crow culture, for instance, did not view themselves as racist. Rather, to the extent that they considered their
status in relationship to blacks, surely they saw themselves as oc-
cupying their particular niche in the great chain of being established not by man (or even men) but by God.

If a state of undeclared, systematic male domination is in fact
the defining characteristic of our culture, we should expect to
find evidence of massive female suffering—chronic as well as
acute—in every quarter. True to form, leading feminists have
produced evidence that such suffering is the female norm.

In her 1992 *Revolution from Within*, Gloria Steinem revealed
that "in this country alone . . . about 150,000 females die of anorexia each year." That is over three times the yearly number of
fatalities from car accidents for the total population. Steinem cites
her comrade-in-oppressed-attractiveness Naomi Wolf, who cites
the statistic in her book *The Beauty Myth*. Wolf is beside herself
with righteous fury. "How," she asks, "would America react to
the mass self-immolation by hunger of its favorite sons?" Although "nothing justifies comparison with the Holocaust," the
temptation proves irresistible. "When confronted with a vast
number of emaciated bodies starved not by nature but by men,
one must notice a certain resemblance.

Wolf got her figures from *Fasting Girls: The Emergence of Anorexia Nervosa as a Modern Disease,* by Joan Brumberg, a historian
and former director of women's studies at Cornell University.
Brumberg declares that the women who study eating problems
"seek to demonstrate that these disorders are an inevitable conse-

quence of a misogynistic society that demeans women . . . by objectifying their bodies." Professor Brumberg attributed the anorexia statistics to the American Anorexia and Bulimia Association.

Christina Hoff Sommers decided to look further. Sommers is the author of the widely acclaimed 1994 book *Who Stole Feminism?* and a former professor of philosophy who has specialized in documenting the slipshod research that has become the cottage industry of feminist ideology. She got on the phone to the American Anorexia and Bulimia Association and spoke to Dr. Diane Mickley, its president. "We were misquoted," she said. The association had referred in a 1985 newsletter to the 150,000 to 200,000 sufferers (not *fatalities*) of anorexia nervosa.

So, what's the correct morbidity rate? Sommers notes that most experts are reluctant to give exact figures. One clinician told her that of 1,400 patients she had treated in ten years, 4 had died—all through suicide. The National Center for Health Statistics reported 101 deaths from anorexia nervosa in 1983, and 67 deaths in 1988. Thomas Dunn of the Division of Vital Statistics at the National Center for Health Statistics says that in 1991 there were 54 deaths from anorexia nervosa and no deaths from bulimia. "The deaths of these young women are a tragedy, certainly, but in a country of one hundred million adult females, such numbers are hardly evidence of a 'holocaust,' " Sommers writes.

Yet now the sham figure, supporting the view that our "women-hating society" degrades women by objectifying their bodies, is generally accepted as true. Ann Landers repeated it in her syndicated column in April 1992: "Every year, 150,000 American women die from complications associated with anorexia and bulimia."

Sommers sent Naomi Wolf a letter pointing out that Dr. Mickley had said she was incorrect. Wolf responded that she intended to revise her figures on anorexia in a later edition of *The Beauty Myth.* "Will she actually state that the correct figure is less than one hundred per year?" Sommers asked. "And will she correct the implications she drew from the false report? For example, will she revise her thesis that masses of young women are being 'starved not by nature but by men' and her declaration that 'women must claim anorexia as political damage done to us by a social order that considers our destruction insignificant . . . as Jews identify the death camps' "?

Don't count on it. The radical feminist belief in the all-pervasive unilateral victimization of women by men has developed the status of a religious tenet that must be taken on faith. "In a patriarchal society all heterosexual intercourse is rape because women, as a group, are not strong enough to give consent." Here Daphne Patai and Noretta Koertge characterize the views of Catharine MacKinnon, which echo Susan Brownmiller's 1975 book *Against Our Will: Men, Women, and Rape,* which infamously declared that all men are potential rapists.

But what does actual human history have to say about women, as a group, and men, as a group? Do we find any convincing evidence that women were ever pawns of a vast patriarchy that keeps them repressed and gives males all the benefits?

Nope.

This answer is grounded in three strikingly succinct facts. First, it turns out males and females are different from one another. Second, nature and culture confer female advantages and male advantages, and likewise confer female disadvantages and male disadvantages. Third, life isn't always fun for either sex. That's the essence of Janet Chafetz's thesis in an exhaustive work of scholarship, *Sex and Advantage.*

Chafetz argues that thousands of years ago women moved from being stick-digging farmers, equal to men in their skills, to being housewives, while the men continued working the field with ox-driven plows. Women made this shift—actually, women and men made it together—because of an increase in the likelihood of miscarriage in the third trimester of pregnancy. Chafetz says it was a "let's continue the species" thing, rather than a "let's keep the chicks barefoot and pregnant" thing. Depending on the ideology you bring to the topic, these may or may not be the same thing. For Chafetz, a sympathetic scholar of feminism, they are *not* the same thing.

Chafetz begins by examining the gender roles of women and men throughout human history—no small task. She finds that in no known societies do men as a group specialize solely in what she calls the "reproductive/private sphere" traditionally occupied by females. Nor in any known society do women as a group specialize exclusively in what she terms the "productive/public sphere" traditionally occupied by males. In all known societies, Chafetz reports, "women's activities are either specialized in nonproductive roles, which leads to inferior status, or divided between the two realms, which may afford them relatively equal status"—in other words, 50–50 at best, and that against the odds.

This leaves Chafetz with the same question as many patriarchy-hating feminists: "Why are women nowhere superior to men in access to scarce and valued societal resources?" That is, why do women never specialize exclusively in productive/public sector roles in any known society? Chafetz reasons that because there are no known exceptions, logically this social fact must be explained in terms of one or more constant factors. She argues that the most obvious constants are *biological,* chiefly the fact that in all human societies "the women carry babies in their bodies and lactate, which circumscribes their physical mobility." While this reality can be minimized (through low birth rates, including via abortion), it cannot be entirely eliminated. "[I]n fact, for most human societies throughout most of human history, such restriction due to pregnancy and nursing has been far from minimal."

Get it? The "oppression" that most enrages radical feminists is imposed not by men but *nature*! Biology, not patriarchy, leads "most societies [to] find it more efficient if women also do the bulk of the caretaking of young children who are no longer nursing." It is "on the basis of expediency [that] the nurturance role is typically extended beyond the biologically based phenomenon of breast-feeding." Notice Chafetz's emphasis on what's most efficient and expedient not for power-hungry males but for nature as such. (Power-hungry males do exist, as do power-hungry females; it's one of those *human* things.)

Back then to Chafetz's query: Why do women never specialize *exclusively* in productive/public sector roles? This is not much different from asking: Why have women tended to stay close to home in all societies? Because "in all the history of our species, women have never been able to divest themselves of some involvement in the reproductive/private sphere of activity," Chafetz concludes. Total divestiture from the constraints of *nature* would be required for women as a group to be free to "monopolize productive/public sector roles," the roles traditionally played by males. (Memo to the National Abortion and Reproductive Rights Action League: How does "Leave No Child Unaborted" sound as a motto that cuts to the chase?)

Patriarchy? For Chafetz, the problem with "oppression" as a causal explanation is that it just doesn't fit the empirical facts.

> [Speculative oppression] theories are based on vaguely defined concepts often ill suited to operationalization, such as "patriarchy," "female subordination," and "sexism." The use of such emotion-laden but unclear terms, combined typically with a heavily normative approach to the topic of sex inequality, results in a maximum of rhetoric but a minimum of clear insight.

That clanking you just heard is the patriarchy theory of human civilization landing in the ashcan of history's bad, wrong, misguided, and just plain silly ideas. Sex roles were designed not by men or women, but by biological necessity, with a strong survival imperative. In a survival-focused world, women needed to be good at raising children. In that same world, men needed to secure the resources to support the biological role of women. Self-fulfillment? Let's just say it wasn't a major priority. Times have obviously changed—in the developed world, at least. Both sexes in America can now rightly focus on striking a balance between survival and self-fulfillment, with unprecedented emphasis on rights and opportunities rather than survival only.

Yet the rhetoric of female victimization by patriarchy—the idea that men rigged the system with rules designed to oppress women—remains the central catechism of feminist faith. If this strikes you as one-sided reasoning, let not your heart be troubled: Males can likewise claim rights to the prized mantle of gender oppression! Yes, there are men's rights activists who argue that it was women who created patriarchy by training young boys to believe it is their sacred duty to make a living doing high-risk jobs like rescuing people from burning buildings and descending into dangerous mines. You see, this makes it possible for wives to outlive their husbands by eight years on average in comfortable homes that the men never got to enjoy because they were preoccupied with living nasty, short, brutish lives.

If this theory strikes you as somewhat misguided—similar to declaring all women to be oppressed by a conspiratorial construct called patriarchy—maybe we're making some progress here. Even so, it would be a fallacy to completely dismiss the idea that men, as men, bear real and legitimate grief in our culture. In fact, the debunking of the patriarchy theory made it possible for me as a journalist to pay attention to reports that I wouldn't have taken seriously back in the days when I casually accepted familiar anecdotes about male violence and female casualties. Quite apart from satire about gender groups competing for advanced victim status, it turns out that female violence and male victimization are also very real—and in ways that simply don't conform to what the patriarchy theory of gender so confidently predicts.

"Forget what you've heard about domestic violence," says Patricia Pearson, author of *When She Was Bad: Violent Women and the Myth of Innocence*. "The truth is that women are just as likely to batter as men."

The largest and most recent survey, conducted three years ago by the U.S. Department of Justice, reported that 39 percent of spousal assault victims are men. Professor John Archer of the University of Central Lancashire in England reached a similar conclusion after analyzing seventeen studies from the United States, Canada, New Zealand, and the United Kingdom published over the last twenty years.

"If you take into account all acts of physical aggression, then there's about equal numbers of men and women being abused," Archer said. He noted that women were more likely than men to receive physical injuries as a result of domestic attacks, but men were equally likely to be victims of less violent forms of abuse.

"The expectation I had was that it was going to be overwhelmingly the women who got injured," Archer continued. "Given that they are more likely to be injured, why is it that they engage in acts of aggression with their partners?" Try this: Violence between males and females is chiefly a human rather than a gender problem.

The first research to show that violence in the home claimed victims of both sexes was conducted over twenty-five years ago by two respected New Hampshire family violence researchers, Richard J. Gelles and Murray A. Straus. They published the results of a survey showing that "women assault their partners at about the same rate as men assault their partners." This applied to both minor and severe assaults. Their findings were published in 1977 as was a book with coauthor Suzanne Steinmetz, Ph.D., in 1980. Responding to feminist criticism of their research methods, Straus and Gelles reworked their questions and sampled several thousand households again. Published in 1985, their findings were virtually identical, with the additional revelation that women initiated the aggression as often as the men. In minor violence (slap, spank, throw something, push, grab, or shove) the incident rates were equal for men and women. In severe violence (kick, bite, hit with a fist, hit or try to hit with something, beat up the other, threaten with a knife or gun, use a knife or gun) more men were victimized than women.

Projecting the surveys onto the national population of married couples, the results showed more than 8 million couples a year engaging in some form of domestic violence, 1.8 million women victims of severe violence, and 2 million male victims of severe violence. The study also found that half of spousal murders are committed by wives.

To say these findings sparked controversy is a colossal under-statement. Feminist activists on the front lines of the domestic violence movement continue to insist that the overwhelming majority (the figure 95 percent is typically cited) of spousal vio-lence cases involve women as victims and men as perpetrators.

"In the rare instances where women behave violently in do-mestic situations, the violence is most often a matter of a woman acting in self-defense," says Donna Garske, executive director of Marin Abused Women's Services, in northern California. "The fundamental cause of partner violence is a belief system in which men are conditioned to expect to have authority over and services from their partners, a worldview which sanctions systematic vio-lence against women."

Researcher David L. Fontes agrees that male partner violence against women is real and must be vigorously challenged. He also says there are far more male victims of spousal violence by women than is widely recognized.

Noting that proponents of the patriarchy theory of domestic

violence often quote a 1977 research study by Murray Straus showing that a woman is severely assaulted by her husband/ boyfriend every fifteen seconds in this country, Fontes says he finds it interesting that the same proponents regularly fail to mention that the same study indicated that a man is severely assaulted by his wife/girlfriend every 14.6 seconds.

"Feminist leaders deserve real credit for rallying around the first women who had the courage to go public with their accounts of being physically assaulted by their male partners," says psychologist Fontes, Employee Assistance Program (EAP) manager for five thousand employees of the California Department of Social Services (CDSS). "Yet many of these leaders seem to be exclusively interested in showcasing the maltreatment of females by males in society. This ignores the clear and convincing body of evidence, numbering more than one hundred well-controlled two-sex studies, which shows there are also male victims of domestic violence by women, independent of self-defense or the evils of patriarchy."

Fontes maintains that the controversy about the ratio of male-to-female victims is fueled by a confusion between two very different kinds of research: archival research (based on data from specialized or clinical sources like police reports, domestic violence centers, hospital ER rooms, and government agencies) and randomized survey research (based on data collected from a randomized sample of the entire population).

"The major problem with archival studies is that they should not be used to make generalizations about the larger population," Fontes says. "Unfortunately, that is exactly what many in the domestic violence movement do with archival data. The serious problem with the claim that ninety-five percent of domestic violence victims are women is that archival data only comes from *reported* cases of domestic violence.

"If there is a population that's less likely to report their victimization, then the archival data is skewed and should not be used to make generalizations from. Research suggests that men are five to nine times *less* likely to report their victimization than women, which will have a major effect on archival results. This is why scientific randomized survey studies are critical in understanding the complete picture of domestic violence."

Lenore Walker, one of the matriarchs of the domestic violence movement, echoes Fontes's concerns about the dangers of using only the reported cases of partner abuse to make generalizations. Of the women she studied for her 1979 book, Walker writes: "These women were not randomly selected and they cannot be considered a legitimate data base from which to make specific generalizations."

In a report called "Violent Touch: Breaking Through the Stereotypes," Fontes reviewed more than one hundred survey-based research studies conducted over the past two decades. He concluded that men and women are assaulting each other at nearly the same rate, or between 35 and 50 percent male victims. Survey data suggest that 50 to 80 percent of domestic violence is *mutual* assault. About 25 percent of the violence is men only, and 25 percent from women only. Women are more likely to receive serious injuries than men, owing to the greater size and strength of men. Only between 10 and 20 percent of women assault their partner for clear reasons of self-defense.

Claudia Dias has seen her share of women and men in both roles, and she's doing her best to reduce the numbers all around. An attorney by training and currently a counselor by practice, Dias is director of Changing Courses, the only authorized treatment program in Sacramento that works with female abusers. She conducts separate weekly anger management groups for women and men.

Dias identified domestic violence "as far more of a family system problem than a power and control problem." She declared that only about 15 percent of the men who assaulted or abused their female partner did so because they felt they had the "male privilege" to do so. "The primary goal of anger and violent behavior"—for male and female perpetrators alike—is to "protect the personal and/or emotional integrity of the perpetrator."

Based on over twenty years of working with perpetrators, both women and men, Dias sees socialization as the main gender distinction. "Women try to keep dialogue going, while men typically walk away and refuse to talk. Men very often say 'I hit her to make her shut up. She just wouldn't shut up.' Women say 'I hit him to make him listen to me. He wouldn't stay and listen, he just walks away.' Different tools, same damage."

Dias says that to grow up female in America is to get a clear message that certain forms of female violence are more than acceptable—they're a sign of virtue. "If a man does or says something offensive, a woman gets to do something without consequence. She gets to slap the man right in the face as hard as she can. We've all seen it. Frank Sinatra propositions a woman who takes offense and hauls off and smacks him. If a woman does this to a man, it's considered a prerogative of her honor. If a man does this to a woman, it's considered an automatic felony. Who do we think we're kidding?"

Warning: My aim in citing the actual facts about domestic violence is decidedly not to set up men as a new class of victims, but instead to show that claims of pervasive male oppressiveness are simply not borne out as we would expect if the patriarchy theory of civilization were accurate. To be sure, men do initiate aggression against women, but women do so as well, and not only in self-defense. I realized the extent to which this turns radical feminist theory for a loop when I spoke with Donna Garske on this subject.

I mentioned to Garske that it seemed plausible that higher rates of male spousal abuse should be expected in communities with military bases. Garske quickly agreed with my statement that males trained to be soldiers are probably more likely to batter their spouses. In fact, no such evidence exists about men in military communities—and I knew that when I made the statement. True confession: I wanted to find out how Garske—an unapologetic proponent of the patriarchy theory—would respond. The clincher came when, in the same experimental spirit, I asked Garske what sense she could make of data showing that spousal abuse takes place among lesbian couples as well as heterosexuals. My question was direct: If men are natural aggressors and women are not, why does so much pummeling take place in lesbian relationships?

"That's an excellent question!" Garske said. "Very perceptive," she added, from which I inferred: unlike most males. "When we find evidence of lesbian battering, the aggressor is taking on the dominator male role, while the victim is assuming the posture that our society demands of the female role, namely victim status."

So there you have it. Males are abusive, and when women abuse other women, they do so . . . as males. Thus the circle remains unbroken; radical feminist theories remain walled off from any possible challenge. But not only in domestic violence. You see, in the all-powerful patriarchy for which mere historical evidence has not yet been discovered, men are likewise the sole perpetrators of abuse against children.

"No one is stating the obvious," Stanford associate professor Carol Delaney declared in a letter to the *San Francisco Chronicle*. Citing the graphic string of high-profile child abductions and murders in recent years, she added: "These hideous crimes are being committed by men."

"What has gone so wrong in the rearing of males in this society?" Delaney asked. "I am disappointed by the silence of decent men who are not taking this on as a men's problem."

Delaney stopped short of saying what's probably on the minds of many cable news viewers these days. Males are violent because violence is masculine; females are the ones who suffer. Conversely, female brutality is rare and almost always unintentional—the result of provocation, mental illness, or various "situational" factors that cause women to believe violence is their only option.

The consensus for these beliefs runs deep in postfeminist America. We could just embrace them as self-evident truths and start from there, except for a niggling complication. The beliefs aren't supported by facts.

To the contrary, empirical data from numerous studies decisively challenges the notion that child abuse in America is exclusively—or even primarily—a men's problem. "Women commit the majority of child homicides in the United States, a greater share of physical child abuse, an equal rate of sibling violence and assaults on the elderly, about a quarter of child sexual abuse, an overwhelming share of the killings of newborns, and a fair preponderance of spousal assaults," writes feminist author and crime journalist Patricia Pearson in her book *When She Was Bad*.

A study by the National Child Abuse and Neglect Data System (NCANDS) found that approximately 879,000 children were victims of child maltreatment in 2000. Based on reports provided by U.S. child protective services agencies, 60 percent of the perpetrators were females and 40 percent were males. The Department of Health and Human Services reached a similar conclusion for the prior year: "Female parents were identified as the perpetrators of neglect and physical abuse for the highest percentage of child victims."

Powerful cultural prejudice works against recognizing abusive women as a widespread malaise. For instance, a Washington state human services professional reported that an accused female offender was brought before a judge who dismissed the case, declaring, "Women don't do things like this." Boston psychologist Laurie Goldman, who analyzed how society minimizes the scale and impact of female sexual abuse, initially located only one woman offender willing to discuss what she had done. Goldman knew from reliable sources that female perpetrators were getting treatment, but clinic administrators insisted that no such women were under their care.

Pearson says women in Western cultures learned to express their bids for power in ways concealed from men. Paradoxically, many women also learned to hide their capacity for aggressive violence from themselves, "as if half the population of the globe consisted of saintly stoics who never succumbed to fury, frustration, or greed," she writes in *When She Was Bad*.

I am not suggesting that men should be let off the hook. Fathers were responsible for 22 percent of sexual abuse in 2000, according to the NCANDS study mentioned above. But of course not all men are child abusers, and Carol Delaney's question waits. Why haven't decent American men as a whole accepted responsibility for the ghastly murders of Polly Klaas and Samantha Runnion?

Probably for the same reason decent American women didn't collectively confess to the wanton killing of Michael and Alex Smith. Remember them? They died horrendous deaths strapped to their car seats after their mother, Susan Smith, deliberately released the emergency brake on her car and let it roll into a South Carolina lake. Smith stood on the shore and watched as the car containing her defenseless sons disappeared under the water's surface.

If David Westerfield's murder of Danielle van Dam is a collective men's problem, does it follow that Smith's drowning of her young sons is a collective women's problem? Not unless we're ready to head down the road to full-blown ideological idiocy.

Still, collective responsibility has its place. As a culture, let's start by recognizing Westerfield and Smith as two faces of the same sadistic beast, concealed by gender wars that will end only when we're ready to see the universal face of human cruelty. In the meantime, maybe a minimum requirement for "decent" persons could be the refusal to exploit the tragedy of exploited children from the sanctuary of great universities.

I'm not at all optimistic that this reform will come from feminism, or that it even can, given how the second wave of feminist thought (in which the systematic powerlessness of women is the transcendent theme) has betrayed first-wave feminism's recognition—which spoke so powerfully to me and other men—that neither women nor men are well served by gender roles that rob women of their full human potential, including their intrinsic capacity for both cruelty and creativity. As Margaret Atwood writes in her novel *Surfacing*: "I have to recant, give up the old belief that I am powerless and because of it nothing I can do will ever hurt anyone."

To embrace this sobering truth would mean an end to the religion of feminism as it has come to exist, but also the birth of something better—ironically, also something older. "The New Feminism emphasizes the importance of the 'women's point of view,' the Old Feminism believes in the primary importance of the human being." Winifred Holtby spoke those words in 1926. If feminism has to be based on faith, give me Holtby's old-time feminist religion any day.

CHAPTER FOUR

THE FALL AND RISE OF CLARENCE THOMAS

Portrait of a Failed Inquisition

I hope [Thomas's] wife feeds him lots of eggs and butter, and he dies early, like many black men do, of heart disease. . . . He's an absolutely reprehensible person.

> —Julianne Malveaux, "progressive" syndicated columnist, November 4, 1994

When President George H. W. Bush nominated Clarence Thomas to the Supreme Court, political intrigue was way off my radar screen. I was busy doing research for a book, housebreaking a beautiful golden retriever puppy, and running central California coastal hills trying to improve my 10K time. Yet the Thomas nomination proved of irresistible interest. Not long after Bush picked the largely unknown member of the D.C. Court of Appeals, I picked up the phone and called an old buddy on Senator Metzenbaum's staff, whom I'll call Jeff.

"Oh, this is going to be a blast," Jeff said when he returned my call, referring to the impending confirmation hearings and his boss's commitment to defeating the nomination. How so? I asked. "Don't you know? Clarence Thomas used affirmative action to get into Yale Law School." I asked Jeff what that meant to him; how did that fact compute?

"If he got a race-based slot, he obviously didn't make it on merit." Pause. Stunned by his frankness, I probed further.

"I thought you favored affirmative action," I said. Longer pause. "I do," Jeff replied. "I'm just saying . . . compared with nonaffirmative action students, Thomas isn't exactly . . . look, don't make me out to be a racist here, I'm just trying to keep a reactionary from making it to the Supreme Court."

The phone call left me furious and feeling betrayed. Clearly the left's religion of diversity had its limits: Black intellectuals were not allowed to hold nonliberal views, not permitted to make social progress without first declaring their primary identity as a racial victim and then lining up for the appropriate reward from the self-marginalizing civil rights establishment, whose very presence increasingly mocked Martin Luther King, Jr.'s quest for a color-blind social policy. Jeff and I agreed on one thing: An epic battle was shaping up. Exactly how would the civil rights community (and more generally the political left) justify opposing a black nominee whom the Senate had confirmed for a district court seat only a year earlier? Would they dare try?

Dare? Who was I kidding? In retrospect, I was approaching the Thomas imbroglio wearing the wrong glasses, the rosy ones. This wasn't a civics class project but an exercise in raw political power on the part of liberal Democrats who still saw the Reagan years as a historical accident. Carter, Mondale, and Dukakis had been lousy candidates, you see, and Reagan, you know, had used his acting skills to, um, fool the American people.

When Thurgood Marshall announced his retirement from the U.S. Supreme Court on the afternoon of June 27, 1991, speculation began not about whether Bush would nominate a black person to fill the seat, but which black person he would choose. Marshall had been the Court's first African American justice, and Bush had considerable incentives to keep the seat black. Just find a qualified black jurist who would pass muster with conservatives, who already felt stung by Bush's earlier choice of closet liberal David Souter.

On July 2, Bush nominated Thomas, calling him the most qualified person in America for the job. Bush (or any other president) would have offered the same accolade to any other nominee, but still: Clarence Thomas? He had been on the district court for just a year, and had not practiced law for a decade prior to that. Conservatives were delighted by Bush's strategy, in effect daring the civil rights community to oppose a black man and a conservative. Thomas was both.

When Thomas got wind that he was being considered, he let it be known that he wasn't interested. He had gone through four confirmation hearings for various federal positions, including as chair of the Equal Employment Opportunity Commission. Having been a member of the D.C. Court of Appeals for only a year, Thomas also knew that key players in the civil rights establishment took strong exception to his opposition to race-based affirmative action programs.

On Monday, July 1, Bush offered Thomas the Supreme Court position. He later told his friend Senator John Danforth: "I was petrified by having to go through the confirmation process and having to live through threats and having to live through people who are poring through files and documents with no purpose other than to destroy you as a person."

Thomas managed to avoid uttering a certain four-letter word: Bork. When Bush nominated Thomas, Florence Kennedy of the National Organization for Women announced at a news conference, "We're going to Bork him. We're going to kill him politically—this little creep. Where did he come from?"

One of America's most distinguished and brilliant legal minds, Robert H. Bork was nominated to the Supreme Court by Ronald Reagan in 1987. Liberals were bound and determined to stop him. Given his stellar record, anti-Bork partisan Ann

Lewis knew a different kind of battle had to be waged. "This had to be fought beyond the walls of the Senate. If this were carried out as an internal Senate battle, we would have deep and thoughtful discussions about the Constitution, and then we would lose." Left-wing advocacy groups joined forces for a smear campaign unprecedented in the history of Supreme Court confirmation battles. Senator Ted Kennedy led with this infamous onslaught:

> Robert Bork's America is a land in which women would be forced into back alley abortions, blacks would sit at segregated lunch counters, rogue police could break down citizens' doors in midnight raids, schoolchildren could not be taught about evolution, writers and artists could be censored at the whim of government, and the doors of the federal courts would be shut on the fingers of millions of citizens for whom the judiciary is—and is often the only—protector of the individual rights that are at the heart of our democracy.

Thomas knew firsthand about an America less polite than Ted Kennedy's Hyannisport. He had grown up in rural Georgia at a time when it was far from unreasonable for a black male to be concerned for his physical survival. He had heard his share of stories about black men who had been abducted and thrown into swamps. Thomas remembered riding in a car as a boy and seeing a billboard that said, THE UNITED KLANS OF AMERICA WELCOMES YOU TO NORTH CAROLINA, and he knew that veering from the interstates onto rural roads could be fatal.

Thomas's past road trips were of scant interest to Democratic congresswoman Eleanor Holmes Norton, the delegate from the District of Columbia, who asked why the president had bothered to nominate a black man at all if he was going to sound like a white. Derrick Bell of Harvard Law School opined that Thomas "doesn't think like a black," and Judge Bruce White of New York characterized Thomas as "emotionally white." Congressman Charles Rangel groused that Thomas "goes against the grain of everything black people believe in" and was "completely against everything that is in the interests of minorities."

Judge Leon Higginbotham, armchair psychiatrist in his free time, diagnosed Thomas as "afflicted with racial self-hatred." To what extent this syndrome overlaps with "Token Black Disorder" is not clear, but that was how *Time* magazine writer Jack White characterized Thomas's affliction. Columbia professor Manning Marable announced that Thomas had "ethnically ceased being an African-American." (Would somebody please tell Clarence?) And there was this charming wisecrack from syndicated columnist Carl Rowan: "If you give Thomas a little flour on his face, you'd think he was David Duke."

Mind you, these are all people who fancy themselves political and cultural *progressives;* apostles of inclusion, tolerance, diversity, and compassion. Remember the days when it was unrepentant white racists who spewed stereotypes like "all colored people look alike"? Queried for dirt on Thomas by staff members for Democratic senators, *Washington Post* columnist Juan Williams wrote: "Here is indiscriminate, mean-spirited mud-slinging supported by the so-called champions of fairness: liberal politicians, unions, civil rights groups and women's organizations. They have been mindlessly led into mob action against one man by the Leadership Conference on Civil Rights."

Had he beaten his first wife? (His former father-in-law repeatedly denied the charge.)

Had he claimed 4-F status to avoid the draft? (Nope; he failed the physical.)

Does he belong to a conservative church where people speak in tongues? (Thomas attended a mainline Episcopal church.)

Did he display a Confederate flag in his office? (Try the Georgia state flag.)

Did he watch porn during law school; did he smoke pot? Had he really shot a man in Reno, just to watch him die? (Wait—that was Johnny Cash, sorry.)

Thomas confided at the time, "These people are going to try to kill me. I hadn't done anything to them, but they are going to try to kill me."

His Senate supporters knew they had their work cut out for them. It was up to Thomas to allay fears about his short tenure on a lower court and his not practicing law for nearly a decade before that.

On September 16, Melissa Riley of Senator Strom Thurmond's staff overheard a conversation between Senator Joe Biden and Judiciary Committee chief counsel Ron Klain.

Klain: "She could testify behind a screen."

Biden: "That's ridiculous. You can't do that. This isn't the Soviet Union."

Deputy White House Counsel Lee Liberman realized that some kind of allegation was floating around about Thomas, but he did not think it was a big deal because Biden wouldn't turn it into something without evidence.

Anita Hill alleged that when she worked at the Department of Education and at EEOC, Thomas had asked her out, she had rejected his overtures, and he had made explicitly sexual remarks to her that included descriptions of pornographic material. Thomas's supporters assumed this charge belonged in the same category as the other scurrilous rumors. In terms of the intrinsic merits of the charges, they had good reason to believe that.

For one thing, the charges were ten years old. Hill had never raised the charges during any of Thomas's previous Senate confirmations—twice as EEOC chairman, once as district court nominee. She had remained silent then, and only came forth at the proverbial last minute, after all other efforts to derail the Supreme Court nomination failed. Did Hill have an ulterior motive? Hill had described differences of opinion with Thomas on proper remedies in civil rights cases. In a court of law, this would be a relevant fact.

Moreover, Hill claimed that after Thomas sexually harassed her at the Department of Education, she followed him to EEOC. Lee Liberman thought this was at least strange. In her analysis, Thomas's opponents would need to find a precedent: "Somebody who has brought a harassment claim where she says, 'I was harassed at Job A, and I nevertheless followed the guy who harassed me to Job B.'"

Judiciary Committee Democrats exercised their option to call for an FBI investigation of Hill's lurid allegations. When FBI agents visited Thomas to inform him of the charges, Thomas couldn't believe what he was hearing. "You've got to be kidding me," he told the agents. "I never had any such conversations with Anita." The larger implications of Hill's charges were immediately clear. "This was the kind of charge . . . she said–he said kind of charge . . . from which I can't clear myself."

Clarence Thomas's days in the slow-pitch leagues were over. This was hardball, and the goal was to knock him out of the game, preferably with a blow to the skull that would serve as a warning to other black conservatives. Civil rights activists have coined the phrase "driving while black" to describe the phenomenon of white police officers arresting black drivers for driving in the wrong (white) neighborhoods at the wrong time (practically any time). "Thinking conservative while black" was Clarence Thomas's crime, and, oh, was this guy going down.

Think *Bork* and then quadruple the effort, because the stakes were so much higher. It was one thing for the liberal establishment to welcome blacks into the American mainstream through racial set-asides designed to keep the recipient aware of his dependence upon the largesse of do-gooders. It was altogether another thing for blacks to get the idea that they could make it on their own in America. Under no circumstances could this be allowed.

Thomas said he hired Anita Hill because she was qualified for the position. A friend of his had vouched for her, and she was a graduate of Yale Law. He hired her as a career attorney rather than as a political attorney. The latter position is partisan; appointees come and go when administrations change. The former is professional, not related to electoral results.

"She was certainly not a Republican," Thomas said. "She was not part of the Reagan team. She was very critical of the administration, critical of me, critical of the people I hired. . . . Her problem essentially was that she could never get over her ideology. In a nutshell, that was her problem, that she saw everything through an ideological glass as opposed to an analytical framework." Thomas described her as "an intelligent black woman" and "a decent person." Her work "wasn't spectacular" and "she was immature and very ideological."

Did Thomas find Hill attractive? If so, that would open the door to the possibility that he may have acted as Hill claimed. Talking with his close friend on the Court of Appeals, Judge Larry Silberman, Thomas said his first reaction to Hill's charges was that "she wasn't attractive at all, and she had bad breath." Thomas's secretary at both the Department of Education and EEOC, Diane Holt, remembers Hill as "always acting like a spoiled brat" and "pouting. . . . Always wanting to have her own way. Always wanting to have the last say."

Thomas recalls, "She would disagree with everybody. . . . When she didn't get her own way, when she was arguing and somebody was getting the better of it, then she would just sort of almost explode. I wouldn't say totally explode. And then she would closet herself in her office."

Pressed as to why she followed Thomas from DOE to EEOC

if she had been sexually harassed, Hill said she went with Thomas reluctantly, fearing the department might be terminated and her job would disappear. Thomas dismisses this as "nonsense." He says that at the time he reminded Hill the Office of Civil Rights in which Hill worked had its own budget, and the OCR would remain intact.

Moreover, Thomas says that both Hill and his secretary specifically asked Thomas if he would take them to his new office at EEOC when Bush appointed him to that position.

Racial politics can be mean. Sexual politics can be vicious. Join the two and something explosively hideous often emerges. For instance, Thomas recalls that when he appointed a black woman, Allyson Duncan, as his new executive assistant, Hill was upset. She complained to Thomas that he had dated a woman with a light complexion, and that Allyson Duncan had a light complexion. Diane Holt says that Hill complained to her that Thomas "likes light women. Or, you never see him with a dark complexioned woman." Hill denied making these statements.

Armstrong Williams, a member of the EEOC staff, saw Hill as a threat, and tried to warn Thomas: "This woman is your mortal enemy, and will do anything to destroy you." Thomas dismissed the warning, saying he felt a "special responsibility" for Hill because his late friend Gil Hardy had asked him to look out for her interests. He said his concern was almost fatherly. "This was sort of like my own child accusing me of something."

My Washington staffer friend Jeff called to say Metzenbaum's staff was becoming nearly obsessed with defeating Thomas. I asked him if it was true that a specific Metzenbaum staffer (whom I named) had leaked the Hill accusations. "No way I can answer that," Jeff said. "But I can tell you this: Metzenbaum is obsessed with defeating Thomas." I asked why. "Your guess is as good as mine. What matters is, Hill's charges are dynamite."

I could scarcely conceal my contempt when I asked Jeff if he meant that the charges were dynamite because of their substance or for their sheer political effect. "It doesn't matter. At this point they're the same thing." I believed he was right about that. I felt a wave of nausea, then something close to rage. It was appalling to hear feminist leaders portray a Yale Law School graduate with a successful government career as a frail, helpless, and powerless victim who could not have been expected to resist (or even report) Thomas's alleged advances at the time they happened. Even if Hill spoke truthfully when she said Thomas had asked her out—even if Thomas talked to Hill about sex—neither act constitutes sexual harassment. Distressed by uninvited references to sex? If so, you're not alone. Whose personal responsibility is it to define what is tolerable and what is not? The responsibility belongs to the person who finds the remarks offensive.

Early feminists demanded an end to double standards by breaking the codes of propriety that protected respectable ladies from foul language and crude behavior. Not every woman today views the resulting liberation as an unquestioned improvement, but those who are happy to be freed from their old status as delicate debutantes are hypocrites when they turn around and demand special treatment. Based on her subsequent friendly behavior toward Thomas, Hill clearly put her career interests above feminist principle.

Let's think together. Anita Hill had the chops to get a law degree from one of the nation's most prestigious law schools, but she couldn't find a convincing way to convey her disapproval and lack of interest in the topics she claimed Thomas raised with her? Hill followed Thomas to a new job place (Thomas said she specifically asked to go with him) and passed up prior confirmation hearings to blow the whistle on him; did ten years need to pass before Hill realized she'd been wronged? His supposed bad behavior suited the workplace culture of EEOC but fell beyond the pale of propriety at the Supreme Court?

Oh, please.

As the Hill-Thomas controversy unfolded, a thirty-three-year-old woman who worked at a shelter for battered women told the *New York Times,* "I was harassed and I nipped it in the bud; I stopped it right then and there. One guy said, 'I see you don't take any guff.'" And a fifty-two-year-old teacher mused, "Wouldn't you haul off and poke a guy in the mouth if he spoke in that manner?"

I personally know women who have been traumatized by the sexual advances of male predators in the workplace. Many of them paid a huge career price by boldly confronting their harassing superiors. Their pain and sacrifice are mocked by feminists who assign heroine status to a woman who lacked the courage to take a stand when the alleged abuse took place.

And then there were the Senate hearings themselves. They amounted to "an atrocious public spectacle worthy of the show trials of a totalitarian regime," says independent feminist Camille Paglia. "Uncorroborated charges about verbal allegations ten years old were paraded on the nation's television screens. The Judiciary Committee should have thoroughly investigated the charges but conducted the proceedings privately. . . . The Senate turned itself into the Roman Collosseum, with decadent, jaded patricians waving thumbs down over a blood-drenched arena."

When Hill's allegations became public, Thomas's agony about why this was happening to him soared. Those closest to him feared he was approaching a complete breakdown. He prayed feverishly for divine guidance and strength. On Friday, October 10, Thomas found the strength to sit down and draft his statement to the committee. He would attempt no formal refutation of Hill on a point-by-point basis, and would speak from his gut. Immediately prior to the hearing, Thomas and his wife, Ginni, and their closest Senate ally, John Danforth of Missouri, crowded into a small room where Danforth, an Episcopal minister, clicked on a

taped rendition of the Mormon Tabernacle Choir singing "On-
ward Christian Soldiers."

As Thomas waited at the witness table for the hearings to
begin, he felt anger rising inside him. Anita Hill had already
detailed her charges. Now it was his turn to speak.

> Mr. Chairman, Senator Thurmond, members of the
> committee: As excruciatingly difficult as the last two
> weeks have been, I welcome the opportunity to clear
> my name today. . . .
>
> The first I learned of the allegations by Professor
> Anita Hill was on September 25, 1991, when the FBI
> came to my home to investigate her allegations. When
> informed by the FBI agent of the nature of the allega-
> tions and the person making them, I was shocked, sur-
> prised, hurt, and enormously saddened.
>
> I have not been the same since that day. For almost a
> decade my responsibilities included enforcing the rights
> of victims of sexual harassment. As a boss, as a friend,
> and as a human being I was proud that I have never had
> such an allegation leveled against me, even as I sought
> to promote women and minorities into nontraditional
> jobs. . . .
>
> I have been wracking my brains and eating my insides
> out, trying to think of what I could have said or done to
> Anita Hill to lead her to allege that I was interested in
> her in more than a professional way, and that I talked
> with her about pornographic or X-rated films. . . .
>
> Throughout the time that Anita Hill worked with me
> I treated her as I treated my other special assistants. I
> tried to treat them all cordially, professionally, and re-
> spectfully. And I tried to support them in their endeav-
> ors, and be interested in and supportive of their success.

I had no reason or basis to believe my relationship with Anita Hill was anything but this way until the FBI visited me a little more than two weeks ago. I find it particularly troubling that she never raised any hint that she was uncomfortable with me. She did not raise or mention it when considering moving with me to EEOC from the Department of Education. And she never raised it with me when she left EEOC and was moving on in her life.

And to my fullest knowledge she did not speak to any other women working with or around me, who would feel comfortable enough to raise it with me, especially Diane Holt, to whom she seemed closest on my personal staff. Nor did she raise it with mutual friends, such as Linda Jackson and Gil Hardy.

This is a person I have helped at every turn in the road since we met. She seemed to appreciate the continued cordial relationship we had since day one. She sought my advice and counsel, as did virtually all of the members of my personal staff.

During my tenure in the executive branch as a manager, as a policy maker, and as a person, I have adamantly condemned sex harassment. There is no member of this committee or this Senate who feels stronger about sex harassment than I do. As a manager, I made every effort to take swift and decisive action when sex harassment was raised or reared its ugly head.

The fact that I feel so very strongly about sex harassment and spoke loudly about it at EEOC has made these allegations doubly hard on me. I cannot imagine anything that I said or did to Anita Hill that could have been mistaken for sexual harassment.

But with that said, if there is anything that I have said

that has been misconstrued by Anita Hill or anyone else to be sexual harassment, then I can say that I am so very sorry and I wish I had known. If I did know I would have stopped immediately and I would not, as I have done over the past two weeks, [have] had to tear away at myself trying to think of what I could have possibly done. But I have not said or done the things that Anita Hill has alleged. God has gotten me through the days since September 25 and He is my judge. . . .

Though I am, by no means, a perfect person, no means, I have not done what she has alleged, and I still do not know what I could possibly have done to cause her to make these allegations.

When I stood next to the president in Kennebunkport, being nominated to the Supreme Court of the United States, that was a high honor. But as I sit here, before you, 103 days later, that honor has been crushed. From the very beginning charges were leveled against me from the shadows—charges of drug abuse, anti-Semitism, wife-beating, drug use by family members, that I was a quota appointment, confirmation conversion, and much, much more, and now this.

I have complied with the rules. I responded to a document request that produced over thirty thousand pages of documents. And I have testified for five full days under oath. I have endured this ordeal for 103 days. Reporters sneaking into my garage to examine books I read. Reporters and interest groups swarming over divorce papers, looking for dirt. Unnamed people starting preposterous and damaging rumors. Calls all over the country specifically requesting dirt. This is not American. This is Kafkaesque. It has got to stop. It must stop for the benefit of future nominees, and our country. Enough is enough.

I am not going to allow myself to be further humiliated in order to be confirmed. I am here specifically to respond to allegations of sex harassment in the workplace. I am not here to be further humiliated by this committee, or anyone else, or to put my private life on display for a prurient interest or other reasons. I will not allow this committee or anyone else to probe into my private life. This is not what America is all about. . . .

Mr. Chairman, in my forty-three years on this Earth, I have been able, with the help of others and with the help of God, to defy poverty, avoid prison, overcome segregation, bigotry, racism, and obtain one of the finest educations available in this country. But I have not been able to overcome this process. This is worse than any obstacle or anything that I have ever faced. . . .

I am proud of my life, proud of what I have done and what I have accomplished, proud of my family, and this process, this process is trying to destroy it all. No job is worth what I have been through, no job. No horror in my life has been so debilitating. Confirm me if you want, don't confirm me if you are so led, but let this process end. Let me and my family regain our lives. I never asked to be nominated. It was an honor. Little did I know that price, but it is too high.

I watched Thomas's testimony with a small group of male and female friends, white and Hispanic, whose political perspective can be accurately described as moderately left of center, essentially sympathetic to women's rights yet none of us hardcore partisans. Few of us believed President Bush's statement that Clarence Thomas was the most qualified nominee in America, yet neither did they consider him unqualified for his conservative views. ("Bush is a Republican," someone said during a commercial. "No surprise he'd nominate a conservative. Democrats nominate liberals. Not exactly rocket science.")

Collectively we had our questions about Anita Hill's claims, particularly the time lag in coming forward publicly. I was decidedly the most political person in the room, known for irony toward political correctness and a withering impression of Ted Kennedy. We were a focus group of sorts, and we were hanging on Thomas's every word. Even the babies in the room—there were three—stopped gurgling as Thomas reached his crescendo.

> I think that this is a travesty. I think that it is disgusting. I think that this hearing should never occur in America. This is a case in which this sleaze, this dirt, was searched for by staffers of members of this committee, was then leaked to the media, and this committee and this body validated it and displayed it in prime time over our entire nation.
>
> How would any member on this committee or any person in this room or any person in this country like sleaze said about him or her in this fashion, or this dirt dredged up, and this gossip and these lies displayed in this manner? How would any person like it?
>
> The Supreme Court is not worth it. No job is worth it. I am not here for that. I am here for my name, my family, my life, and my integrity. I think something is dreadfully wrong with this country, when any person, any person in this free country, would be subjected to this. This is not a closed room.
>
> There was an FBI investigation. This is not an opportunity to talk about difficult matters privately or in

a closed environment. This is a circus. It is a national disgrace. And from my standpoint, as a black American, as far as I am concerned, it is a high-tech lynching for uppity blacks who in any way deign to think for themselves, to do for themselves, to have different ideas, and it is a message that, unless you kowtow to an old order, this is what will happen to you, you will be lynched, destroyed, caricatured by a committee of the U.S. Senate, rather than hung from a tree.

When Thomas stopped speaking, someone picked up the clicker and turned down the volume. The room was silent for at least thirty seconds. And I knew from the collective silence that Thomas would emerge victorious; we all knew. Thomas had already achieved his triumph, regardless of the Senate's vote. It was one of the most powerful moments I have witnessed on television to this day, different from yet comparable in spirit to Martin Luther King, Jr.'s "I Have a Dream" speech.

King aspired to a society where blacks are judged by "the content of their character." Thomas asserted his "right to think for myself, to refuse to have my ideas assigned to me as though I was an intellectual slave because I'm black." Self-styled progressives once chased to embrace the message at the heart of this vision; now they chase away those who espouse it. Today's reactionary liberals use multicultural and gender correctness just as Sheriff Bull Connor used vicious police dogs and water cannons: to keep free people in their place. Now as then, good people refused to stay put. They kept moving. They're moving still, leaving the left to its mastery of righteous misery and irrelevant rage.

CHAPTER FIVE

THE RIGHT TO KILL NEWBORNS

Partial-Birth Abortion and the Error Called *Roe*

SEN. SANTORUM: *If the baby was delivered accidentally, and the head slipped out, would you allow the doctor to kill the baby?*

SEN. LAUTENBERG: *I am not making the decision.*

—U.S. Senate debate, September 26, 1996

To this day I can't say which was more chilling: their words or their tone, or somehow the combination. On the floor of the United States Senate, televised by C-SPAN, Rick Santorum (R-Pennsylvania) and his colleagues Frank Lautenberg (D-New Jersey) and Russ Feingold (D-Wisconsin) were discussing the procedure known as partial-birth abortion. Santorum pointed to a poster depicting an abortionist inserting a syringe into the base of a baby emerging from its mother's birth canal, then using the syringe to suction out the baby's brains. Then Santorum asked Lautenberg a question.

"If that baby at twenty-four weeks was delivered accidentally, just like that, but instead of the head being held in by the physician, the head was accidentally delivered, by mistake, would the doctor and the mother have a right to kill that baby?"

"My colleague from Pennsylvania can cloak it in any terms," Lautenberg responded. Had he not understood the plain meaning of Santorum's words?

"Answer the question," Santorum said.

"Well, no, frame your question," Lautenberg insisted.

"If the baby was delivered accidentally, and the head slipped out, would you allow the doctor to kill the baby?"

"I am not making the decision," Lautenberg said.

"But that's what we are doing here, Senator, we are making decisions," Santorum said.

Lautenberg replied, "You are making decisions that say a doctor doesn't have . . ."

"So two inches make the difference as to whether you'll answer that question?"

"No, what makes the difference is someone who has the knowledge and intelligence and experience making the decision, as opposed to a graphic demonstration that says this is the way we are going to do it," Lautenberg said.

Santorum, who opposes partial-birth abortions, continued the conversation with Feingold, who believes the decision about whether to perform the procedure should be left up to the mother and the doctor.

"My question is this," Santorum said, "that if that baby were delivered breech style and everything was delivered except for the head, and for some reason that baby's head would slip out—that the baby was completely delivered—would it then still be up to the doctor and the mother to decide whether to kill that baby?"

"I would simply answer your question by saying under the Boxer amendment, the standard of saying it has to be a determination, by a doctor, of the health of the mother, is a sufficient standard that would apply to that situation," Feingold said. "And that would be an adequate standard."

Santorum wasn't satisfied. "That doesn't answer the question.

Let's assume that this procedure is being performed for the reason that you've stated, and the head is accidentally delivered.
Would you allow the doctor to kill the baby?"

"I'm not the person to be answering that question," Feingold
said. "That is a question that should be answered by a doctor, and
by the woman who receives advice from the doctor. And neither
I, nor is the Senator from Pennsylvania, truly competent to answer those questions. That is why we should not be making those
decisions here on the floor of the Senate."

I quote these exchanges at some length because when I watched
the debate live via C-SPAN I found the responses of Lautenberg
and Feingold beyond astonishing. Playing back the exchange on
videotape, I turned up the volume thinking I might hear some
shift in the senators' voices to indicate that they really meant to
say: No. Neither a doctor nor the mother would have the right to
kill a living baby. But there was no change of tone, no catching of
the breath, no modified gesture from either Lautenberg or Feingold to suggest that the content of the conversation was different
from a 1950s government training film on the effective laying of
asphalt.

It took me some time to realize that the real shift had been taking place in both my heart and mind in subtle yet insistent ways.
My position on abortion had been changing in the wake of decid-
ing to restart a process that had stopped a good many years earlier, called thinking, specifically the act of examining a few basic
conclusions that had crystallized at an earlier stage of my life and
had remained unexamined. Precisely by not being questioned, my
assumptions about a host of abortion issues—first, the intrinsic
moral issues related to life; second, the jurisprudence of *Roe v.
Wade*—eventually claimed a degree of inner authority based more
on ideology fueled by emotion than on critical reasoning.

I was a nineteen-year-old college freshman when the Court issued its *Roe* ruling. Politically liberal and a supporter of civil and legal equality for women, I hadn't given any serious thought to abortion as such, let alone to the two sides of the issue or even to the idea that two "sides" existed. When the feminist contingent within the overall liberal coalition celebrated *Roe* as a great freedom event for women and a definite mark of social evolution, I didn't question their conclusion. For one thing, abortion was a women's issue; what business did a man have opposing abortion? The right to control one's own body made sense; back-alley abortions did not. Abortion will continue to happen; let's make sure they happen safely. I became pro-choice and expressed my commitment by participating in more than one national demonstration in support of a woman's right to choose.

For a long time I simply took for granted that, as abortion-rights activists claim, there exists a general right to privacy in the Constitution. Therefore, it followed that the right to abortion is constitutionally grounded. Moreover, though I had never sat down to read the Supreme Court's *Roe v. Wade* decision from beginning to end, I accepted as true the widespread belief that this famously controversial ruling allows for unrestricted abortion rights only during the first trimester of pregnancy.

When does life begin? I said I didn't know for sure. It's up to every pregnant woman to decide this question for herself. Though appalled by the seeming callousness of Lautenberg/Feingold's "let the doctor and mom decide," I had to admit I probably would have given a similar answer myself, at a different time in my life.

I remember responding to an antiabortion activist who insisted that my agnosticism about when life begins amounted to a fundamental cop-out. I can still feel the tinny hollowness of my strained response: "It's up to each woman to decide for herself." Raising the specter of criminalization, I demanded to know whether the pro-life activist would jail women for having an abortion. It comes down to a basic right to freedom, I said. I believed that at the time I supported and accepted the legitimacy of *Roe v. Wade*. I still believe the issue of freedom is paramount. Today, however, I come down on the side of the liberty rights of those whom Kate O'Beirne calls "the smallest humans," unborn children.

Moreover, I now believe *Roe* should be overturned and the right to choose expanded in this sense: Abortion should be decided through the political process, through legislatures rather than courts. Ironically, the voices that most influenced me to rethink this issue were pro–abortion rights activists who took a close look at the logic of *Roe v. Wade* and came away holding their noses and grimacing. Though in one sense separable, the matters of *how* Roe was decided and what Roe *declared* are inextricably bound. For, contrary to widely held beliefs, exemptions within the trimester system formulated by *Roe* actually permit unrestricted abortion for any reason all the way up to viability. Indeed, under the prevalent reading of slapdash language in *Roe*'s companion case, *Doe v. Bolton,* abortion in the period from viability until birth is not forbidden.

But, again: Who is to decide the fate of a fetus in the womb of a woman who claims autonomy? Is not abortion significantly a freedom issue, a matter of unalienable rights as set forth in the Declaration of Independence? For me the answer is decidedly yes—but now my thoughts and sympathies lie with "the smallest humans" who escaped the attention of Lautenberg and Feingold. The Founders understood nothing so clearly as this: Our rights are not granted by government. Rather, the duty of government is to secure our rights to "life, liberty, and the pursuit of happiness." In this sense our unalienable rights are prepolitical. Pro-choice activist Nadine Strossen, president of the American Civil Liberties Union (ACLU), puts the matter this way: "We don't need the Ninth Amendment or the Constitution to have rights; we have rights by virtue of the fact we are human beings."

Neither the Declaration nor the Constitution that enshrines its core ideas establishes a two-tiered legal policy on human beings that defines a superior class as persons with rights and an inferior class without rights. The question of personhood, and of the humanity of the preborn child, is at the very heart of the abortion issue. I once took refuge in the belief that we cannot say with certain when human life begins. I now view that as a mistaken question. The real issue is: When does the life of every human *being* begin? Fact: The human embryonic organism formed at fertilization is not a potential or a possible human being but an actual human being with the potential to grow bigger and develop its capacities.

If the Declaration of Independence got it right, that we are created equal and are endowed by our Creator with an unalienable right to life, does this warrant significant governmental protection of the lives of unborn human beings? For me the answer is yes.

Does the prenatal child have the right to be in the mother's womb? Again, yes. Amazingly, the philosopher-god named Harry Blackmun assumed in *Roe* the existence of potential life, a special category of human offspring that lies somewhere between nonperson and person. With the increasing physical development of human beings comes a growing moral standing and, hence, an increasing level of rights, until at some point in our development, we acquire full rights.

This raises the awful question that Lautenberg and Feingold were understandably eager to skirt. Since human beings do not mature until adulthood, what's wrong with infanticide? Apparently sensing the need to apply the brakes, Blackmun wrote, "With respect to the State's important and legitimate interest in potential life, the 'compelling' point is at viability. This is so because the fetus then presumably has the capability of meaningful life outside the mother's womb." But what is meaningful, and by whose criteria? In common language, viable means capable of living or developing in normal or favorable situations. To abortionists, viable requires survivability under hostile conditions. Either way, what is the connection between viability and what an entity is, or with the right not to be killed?

If you need help, you can be killed, but if you can manage, you cannot be touched, so the Court seemed to say. The *more* a child needs the womb, the *less* right she has to stay there; this is the Court's hidden message. Even so, let's accept viability as the key factor. To do so is to be forced to acknowledge that viability is not a stable point. Since *Roe* the age at which prematurely born children survive in incubators has lowered markedly. As Justice Sandra Day O'Connor wrote, "The *Roe* framework, then, is clearly on a collision course with itself."

Simply stated, Blackmun confused technological medical problems with philosophical ones. Viability is not a measure of personhood; it is a measure of the state of medical technology and of the competence of medical personnel. A hospital that lacks the ability to maintain a life does not confer upon them or anyone else a right to take that life. Their particular inability can have no bearing on whether another's death is a homicide or not.

Law professor Richard A. Epstein—a libertarian who values freedom and opposes the encroachment of the state on human rights—called the Court's stand on viability astonishing, insisting that *Roe* places no meaningful barrier against abortion even after viability.

> [T]he Court holds that the state is entitled, but not required, to protect its, the unborn child's, interest. The reason for the entitlement is that the fetus is now capable of an independent life outside the mother. But the problem is, why should not the claims of the fetus [between viability and birth] be sufficiently strong to

require, and not merely to permit, the state to intervene for its protection? After the Court expressed such firm views on the proper balance [between the claims of the woman against those of the fetus] until the onset of viability, it gave no explanation why the state must be allowed to make its own choice after that time.

Epstein is not alone in his conviction that *Roe* is deeply antagonistic to core precepts of American government and citizenship. More than a few pro-choice advocates agree that by at once nationalizing abortion and removing it from the political process, *Roe* prevented Americans from working together, through a continuous process of peaceful and vigorous persuasion, to formulate and revise the policies on abortion governing our fifty states.

It is hard to find a more liberal law professor in America than Harvard's Laurence H. Tribe. Here's his verdict: "One of the most curious things about *Roe* is that, behind its own verbal smokescreen, the substantive judgment on which it rests is nowhere to be found."

Or Edward Lazarus, a law clerk to Justice Harry Blackmun who describes himself as "someone utterly committed to the right to choose [abortion]" and as "someone who loved *Roe*'s author like a grandfather." Lazarus declares, "As a matter of constitutional interpretation and judicial method, *Roe* borders on the indefensible." He adds: "Justice Blackmun's opinion provides essentially no reasoning in support of its holding. And in the almost thirty years since *Roe*'s announcement, no one has produced a convincing defense of *Roe* on its own terms."

Watergate special prosecutor Archibald Cox, fired by Richard Nixon for doing his job to ferret out high-level corruption, is unflinching in his criticism. "[*Roe*'s] failure to confront the issue in principled terms leaves the opinion to read like a set of hospital rules and regulations. . . . Neither historian, nor layman, nor lawyer will be persuaded that all the prescriptions of Justice Blackmun are part of the Constitution."

Justice Ruth Bader Ginsburg has raised similar concerns about *Roe,* saying the monumental decision went too far, too fast, and reached its conclusion for all the wrong reasons. Though she supports the right to abortion, Bader had this to say: "*Roe,* I believe, would have been more acceptable as a judicial decision if it had not gone beyond a ruling on the extreme statute before the court. . . . Heavy-handed judicial intervention was difficult to justify and appears to have provoked, not resolved, conflict."

Justice Byron White expressed similar concerns in his forceful 1973 dissent to the Court's *Roe* holding:

> At the heart of the controversy in these cases are those recurring pregnancies that pose no danger whatsoever to the life or health of the mother but are, nevertheless, unwanted for any one or more of a variety of reasons—convenience, family planning, economics, dislike of children, the embarrassment of illegitimacy, etc. . . .
>
> With all due respect, I dissent. I find nothing in the language or history of the Constitution to support the Court's judgment. The Court simply fashions and announces a new constitutional right for pregnant mothers and, with scarcely any reason or authority for its action, invests that right with sufficient substance to override most existing state abortion statutes. . . . As an exercise of raw judicial power, the Court perhaps has authority to do what it does today; but, in my view, its judgment is an improvident and extravagant exercise of the power of judicial review that the Constitution extends to this Court.
>
> The Court apparently values the convenience of

the pregnant mother more than the continued existence and development of the life or potential life that
she carries. Whether or not I might agree with that
marshaling of values, I can in no event join the Court's
judgment because I find no constitutional warrant for
imposing such an order of priorities on the people and
legislatures of the States. In a sensitive area such as
this, involving as it does issues over which reasonable
men may easily and heatedly differ, I cannot accept
the Court's exercise of its clear power of choice by in-
terposing a constitutional barrier to state efforts to
protect human life and by investing mothers and doctors with the constitutionally protected right to exterminate it.

Regardless of one's views on the *political* question of whether
abortion should be legal, or the *moral* questions about life and
death, *Roe* is bad law and bad policy, because it expands the
power of the federal government beyond its rightful bounds. "All
power to the people" was perhaps the most basic article of my
early liberal faith. I hadn't studied constitutional theories of state-
federal relations, yet clearly the continuous encroachment of the
national government on state and local authority posed a fundamental threat to the sovereignty of the people. I came away from
the Cuyahoga Valley and Big Sur land battles profoundly suspi-
cious of the standard liberal faith in federal decision making. Because human knowledge is always partial and therefore fallible,
local small-scale action creates less potential for negative consequences.

The scale doesn't get much smaller, nor the implications of
potential action more clear, than watching a live image of your
not yet born child's heart beating. My son's heart began to thump
with his own blood by the twenty-second day after fertilization,

which was also day one of his human journey, because all of his chromosomes were present and his unique life initiated. At week five, his eyes, legs, and hands began to develop. Little more than a month later, Skyler's teeth began forming, and his fingernails developing. He was able to turn his head, and frown. He could hiccup.

By the completion of the first trimester he had all the body parts required to feel pain, including nerves, spinal cord, and thalamus. Vocal cords were complete. He could suck his thumb, and I watched him do this on the screen in a room filled with high-tech equipment and the enraptured silence of his dad and mom.

During the final two months of pregnancy my son could open and close his eyes and use four of the five senses: vision, hearing, taste, and touch. He was able to recognize the difference between waking and sleeping, able as well to relate to the moods of his mom. Skyler's skin began to thicken, and a layer of fat developed beneath the skin. Antibodies built up, and his heart began to pump three hundred gallons of blood per day. Approximately one week before the birth my son stopped growing (which is normal) and dropped head down into the pelvic cavity.

Let's put aside what's morally right, just for a moment. Should his mother and I have had the legal right to tell the attending physician in the delivery room that we had changed our minds; could he please use the forceps to crush our son's skull and deposit his lifeless body in whatever means he found consistent with his Hippocratic oath to "do no harm"?

Of course not. Human offspring are persons from conception. If any class of persons deserves the right to be deemed innocent, prenatal children most assuredly do. The proper purpose of the law is to side with the innocent, not against them. I had a clear moral obligation to do everything I could to help secure my son's right to be inside his mom's body. A society in full possession of its faculties would recognize no right—legal, constitutional, moral, spiritual—to evict unborn children from the womb and let them die.

Skyler came into this world healthy and whole around one in the morning on the second day of a new year, following a long and arduous labor. After bonding with Mom (including getting the hang of breast-feeding), my son slept next to me that first morning of our life together. I stayed awake and watched him. In the months that followed, I stayed awake and walked him—a lot. There is nothing quite like a crying baby at midnight to make you realize just how expendable sleep can be.

Back now to the Senate floor. Senators Lautenberg and Feingold: Are you with the majority of your fellow Americans on this? Give it some thought and get back to us. We need to know your answer. It's really important.

CHAPTER SIX

NONE DARE CALL IT PERJURY

The Serial Shams of Boomer Bill Clinton

I did not have sexual relations with that woman.

—William Jefferson Clinton, January 26, 1998

Dear Bill: Thanks for the lies—all of 'em. The brilliant ones and the stupid ones. The tiny ones and the bald-faced ones. The whoppers and the wink-of-the-eye lies. The graded lies and the shaded lies, the follow-up lies aimed to anchor the earlier lies. Oh, sure— part of me wishes you hadn't been so chronically untruthful. An even bigger part wishes you hadn't committed the sad and some- times seemingly psychotic wrongful acts that made all the lies necessary in your mind. I say this as someone who voted for you twice and admired your work as chairman of the Democratic Leadership Council at a time when your party seemed to have lost its capacity for responsible discourse.

Thanks, too, for the timing of your key fabrications and fail- ures of moral courage. Your avalanche of lies corresponded to a key event in my personal life, and, well, I'm kind of a sucker for synchronicities. The House of Representatives voted to impeach you in the days just prior to the birth of my son. Around this time your key supporters had perfected the novel defense that lying under oath doesn't count as perjury when the lies have to do with sex. Of course, I realize you still don't think what you had with "that woman" constituted sex—she was having sex with you! (Where were you when I needed this kind of thinking in high school?) But the grand jury said you did, and most Americans think you did, and I do, too.

My son is relevant here precisely in this way. When you were busy denying responsibility for your actions—serially disgracing yourself, your wife and daughter, your staff, supporters, and friends—I was having some of those first conversations that a first-time dad has with a newborn; the walking around in the middle of the night discussions about the life you hope he'll have—like, if he ever stops crying and lets the both of you get some rest. Those mentor-to-protégé soliloquies about the sort of nation you hope he'll inherit, the manner of decisions he'll make, the uncharted frontiers he may choose to explore. Because I love politics and believe its practice can engage what Lincoln called "the better angels of our nature," one particular night I told my baby boy that I hoped he would care enough about his country to want to take on with enthusiasm the highest office available in a democracy, namely, citizen.

Back to lies: I've told a few over the years—you'd get a kick out of some of my more inspired convolutions. My kid's in grade school now, and you won't be surprised to hear that he's already developed considerable spin talent of his own. Because he's blessed with free will, he'll have lifelong choices to make about his relationship with truth, reality, and creativity. So I write this chapter especially for my son and his generation. I'm hoping they might benefit from your example, by not emulating it—how not to treat their friends and allies, how not to behave either in public or private, how not to forget that whatever wrong thing they may do, lying and misleading and covering up only make things worse. Oh, I know you're probably tired of serving as an object lesson, but consider the bright side: At least I'm *talking* about you, and

I know that counts for a lot in the inordinately self-regarding psyche of Bill Clinton.

So, this last note of gratitude. Kudos for the work you've done to pass on your skills to Hillary. A lot of husbands hog their talents, but you obviously care enough about empowering women (I'm not being facetious here, Mr. President) to be willing to mentor Hillary in the fine points of mendacity. Sure, she lacks your imagination and emotional range, but she's got this great *earnestness* thing going, and though it doesn't quite make up for the absence of normal mammalian qualities, it has its place in the practice of prevarication!—KT.

I liked Bill Clinton when he and Hillary first introduced themselves to the American public in their famous January 26, 1992, interview with *60 Minutes* correspondent Steve Croft. The Clintons appeared together as Bill responded to Gennifer Flowers's lurid account (in the supermarket tabloid the *Star*) of a twelve-year love affair with the candidate. According to the *Wall Street Journal*, Flowers was paid upwards of $140,000 for her story.

Croft asked Bill Clinton about Flowers's accusation. "That allegation," he replied firmly, "is false." In response to a backup question, Clinton said that both he and Flowers herself had previously denied the affair. He went on famously to acknowledge having "caused pain in my marriage," and added that he trusted voters to understand what he meant by that, and indicated that he and Hillary would have nothing more to say about it.

In effect, Clinton admitted adultery. At least he's not denying it, I thought to myself. When Hillary added that she and her husband had worked out their problems and had chosen to recommit themselves to their marriage, it seemed to me they deserved some credit for hanging together through hard times. In a subsequent ABC News poll, 73 percent of respondents said they agreed with

Clinton that whether or not he'd ever had an extramarital affair was between him and his wife. Six months later Clinton seemed to me to show some courage by angering Jesse Jackson in the process of criticizing a rap artist named Sister Soulja.

Speaking at one of Jesse Jackson's Rainbow Coalition shindigs, Clinton said:

> You had a rap singer here last night named Sister Soulja. I defend her right to express herself through music, but her comments before and after Los Angeles were filled with a kind of hatred that you do not honor today and tonight. Just listen to this, what she said. She told the *Washington Post* about a month ago, and I quote, "If black people kill black people every day, why not have a week and kill white people?" Last year she said, "You can't call me or any black person anywhere in the world racist. We don't have the power to do to white people what white people have done to us. And even if we did, we don't have that lowdown, dirty nature. If there are any good white people, I haven't met them."

If candidate Clinton could be courageous, as president he opted for craven more often than not. After entering the White House, Bill Clinton increasingly struck me as the kind of guy you wouldn't want to be in a foxhole with, not with enemy fire flying all around. In 1993 he nominated Lani Guinier to head the Justice Department's civil rights enforcement efforts—then yanked her nomination when critics challenged her views on voting rights. During the campaign Clinton pledged to do for gays what Harry Truman had done for blacks in 1948—eliminate the military's discriminatory policies by executive order, starting a social revolution with the stroke of a pen. Fifteen months later, faced with widespread opposition in the ranks and stonewalling from the

Joint Chiefs of Staff, Clinton retreated. On issue after issue Bill Clinton seemed more prepared to back down rather than fight for principle, making clear his willingness to split the difference with his opponents before the battle had grown fierce, or in some cases before the battle had even begun.

So by the time Clinton faced the Lewinsky crisis in 1998, my expectations weren't very high. Even so, the question on my mind was the same question millions of Clinton supporters were asking: If he has nothing to hide, then why is he hiding? As the president failed to respond to the growing evidence of wrongdoing, it became increasingly difficult to extend the benefit of the doubt. A person innocent of what Clinton was accused of doing would not wait for the subpoena that finally compelled him to speak, nor would he invoke executive privilege as a way to hide relevant facts. And he wouldn't raise his hand to tell the truth and then utter Monty Pythonesque circularities about what constitutes a sex act.

CLINTON ACCUSED OF URGING AIDE TO LIE. So blared the *Washington Post* on Wednesday morning, January 21, 1998. On the previous Friday three federal judges had authorized independent counsel Kenneth W. Starr to enlarge the scope of an existing investigation in order to look into allegations of suborning perjury, making false statements under oath, and obstructing of justice. Each criminal allegation directly concerned President Clinton. America subsequently learned of the president's illicit involvement with a twenty-one-year-old intern named Monica Lewinsky.

The story churned for several days, and despite prompt denials from Clinton, the cry for answers from the White House grew louder. On January 26, a visibly upset President Clinton addressed the public in a White House press conference and issued a vigorous denial:

> Now, I have to go back to work on my State of the Union speech. And I worked on it until pretty late last

night. But I want to say one thing to the American people. *I want you to listen to me. I'm going to say this again. I did not have sexual relations with that woman, Miss Lewinsky* [emphasis added]. I never told anybody to lie, not a single time; never. These allegations are false. And I need to go back to work for the American people.

When President Clinton gave his deposition in the Paula Jones sexual harassment case, he reiterated this remarkable claim that he had never had "sexual relations" with Monica Lewinsky, even though Lewinsky had testified in detail about performing oral sex on Clinton in the Oval Office. Explaining to Starr's grand jury why his lawyer said at the Jones deposition that there "is absolutely no sex of any kind" between Clinton and Lewinsky, Clinton testified: "It depends on what the meaning of the word 'is' is . . . actually, in the present tense, that is an accurate statement."

This led his questioner to ask mockingly: "Do you mean today that because you were not engaging in sexual activity with Ms. Lewinsky during the deposition that the statement . . . might be literally true?"

When Clinton was asked to explain his statement in the Jones case that he did not recall being alone with Lewinsky, he said, "There were a lot of times when we were alone, but I never really thought we were."

The president's defenders took a more pragmatic approach. Conceding that sex had in fact taken place, they argued that the case was *only* about sex. CNN *Crossfire* host Bill Press crystallized what was to become the core of team Clinton's public relations strategy. "With . . . one admission, Monica Lewinsky exposes the total absurdity of the entire Starr investigation: It's about sex." From there, the argument evolved: A president's private sexual behavior is none of the nation's business. Thus began a campaign of special pleading for boy Bill by a growing chorus of adult enablers.

Washington Post columnist Mary McGrory wrote of "the simple truth that has been apparent to the man and the woman in the street from day one: reprehensible is not impeachable. Americans would prefer a monogamous husband. But . . . they are not going to insist on it. Monkey business in the Oval Office just doesn't make the constitutional standard of 'high crimes and misdemeanors.' " Geraldo Rivera said he was "sure something probably happened" between Bill Clinton and Monica Lewinsky, but even assuming the president had done everything he was accused of, at worst "he's a hypocrite. So what? Get over it." Democratic Party operative (and big-time feminist) Susan Estrich asked, "Should allegedly finding comfort, release, satisfaction, peace in the arms of a beautiful twenty-one-year-old count for more than balancing the budget?"

After all, Bill Clinton had long since acknowledged that he had "caused pain in his marriage." Hillary said she had long since forgiven him. And so the post-Lewinsky defense ensued: If the president's wife forgives him, who are we to judge the guy? Social critic Wendy Kaminer, whose book *A Fearful Freedom* sneered at women who choose the role of mother first over working outside the home, put it this way: "Why should we hold the president to standards of moral behavior that few of us meet consistently? . . . I'm not suggesting that the president's lies and infidelities don't matter. They must matter a lot to Hillary and Chelsea Clinton. But why should they matter to voters?" High-profile lawyer Gerry Spence, famous for defending Randy Weaver in the Ruby Ridge incident, insisted that the investigation amounted to little more than a "panty raid."

Clinton's inner circle turned their biggest guns on Kenneth Starr. "These people [the office of independent counsel] are obsessed with sex," declared James Carville. "This thing is totally out of control. . . . He's [Starr] a sex-obsessed person who's out to get the president. . . . He's concerned about three things: sex, sex, and more sex. That's all the man's about. . . . It's about sex."

The defense was laughable not least because Clinton's baby-boom defenders came of age politically during the Watergate era. Nixon's self-serving claim that the Watergate scandal was about nothing more than a "third-rate burglary" didn't accept the implication that only a first-rate burglary would be cause for concern. Nixon's investigators painstakingly showed that his crimes were the inexorable result of a political culture fostered and nurtured in stonewalling, half-truths, evasions, deliberate distortions, obstruction of justice, and assorted skullduggery. Over time, however, activists who decried Nixon's abuses of power—including Hillary Clinton, who served as a young staffer to the Senate Watergate committee—discovered that holding political power is even more fun than condemning its abuses from behind the ivy-covered walls of college campuses.

These activists were the descendants of the rock musical *Hair,* with its celebration of the Age of Aquarius, a promising new era based on harmony and understanding, free of past "falsehoods" and "derisions," a time when the human mind would be liberated by "mystic crystal revelations." The controversial stage production was performed by nude actors celebrating orgiastic, drug-enhanced evasion of reality and contempt for the established order. Expelled from high school, a character named George reviles the educational hierarchy, while Claude, who has gotten a draft notice, launches into an anthem in which he declares that he will never cut his "long beautiful hair, shining, streaming, flaxen, waxen." So goes the revelry as draft cards are burned and cares float away on wafting clouds of marijuana smoke.

Not every person born between 1946 and 1964 (the baby-boomer era) was captured by the narcissistic spirit of entitlement and self-satisfied revolutionary zeal that characterizes popular associations with that era; yet it is hard to doubt that Bill Clinton personifies a generation-wide belief that they represented a truly new paradigm of societal evolution.

"We" represent freeing the human spirit from the old culture of greed, dogma, divisiveness, hierarchy, and abuses of power.

"We" place caring over the dictates of impersonal rationality.

"We" cherish the earth, Gaia, life itself.

"We" believe in reaching decisions through reconciliation and consensus, compassion and equality.

"We" know the value of nonlinear thinking to achieve win-win solutions.

"We" personify warmth, sensitivity, vision.

"We" ended the war in Vietnam, "we" drove Nixon from office, "we" pioneered in civil rights, feminism, ecology, and diversity.

Recycling—did "we" mention recycling; "we" invented that too. "We" are one frigging, amazing, unprecedented generation!

Deeply convinced that these "we are the world, watch us sway" convictions imbue their daily undertakings with righteousness, Clinton defenders accordingly managed to persuade themselves that their guy's breaking of the rules didn't truly qualify as violations. Or to put it another way, their grandiose Aquarian self-esteem made it possible to rationalize breaking the rules (including breaking the law) because they are, you see, deeply committed to a new kind of society, of which they themselves happen to be the chief exemplars. Philosopher Ken Wilber has satirized this psychological syndrome of supersaturated self-importance as "boomeritis." Here's his take on the Aquarius generation's "discovery," for instance, of *dialogue* as a virtue:

> To hear the boomeritis version, which has appeared in literally thousands of publications, nobody seems to have really understood the importance of dialogue

When 8.5 million Iraqis participated in their first free election and liberals could find nothing nice to say about it, my long-growing estrangement from the left was cemented.
(Photograph by Brent Stirton/Getty Images)

I'd been a lifelong Democrat, even a staffer for the liberal Ohio senator Howard Metzenbaum, whose refusal to defend homeowners from a tyrannical federal government landgrab, in the name of eminent domain, shook my faith in the left's claim to speak for ordinary people.
(Photograph by Ron Sachs/Consolidated News Pictures/Getty Images)

Supreme Court justice Harry Blackmun's 1978 argument for reverse racism ("In order to treat some persons equally, we must treat them differently") made clear to me that the left had abandoned Martin Luther King, Jr.'s call for an America that would judge its citizens by the content of their character rather than the color of their skin.
(Photograph by Cynthia Johnson/Liaison/Getty Images)

Almost thirty years later, self-aggrandizing demagogues such as Al Sharpton represent what it means to be liberal about race in America.
(Photograph by Carlo Allegri/Getty Images)

Watching the left's campaign of character assassination against Supreme Court nominee Clarence Thomas opened my eyes to the hypocrisy of today's civil rights establishment, which embraces "diversity" except when black conservatives dare to think for themselves.
(Photograph by J. David Ake/AFP/Getty Images)

Anita Hill, accusing Thomas of having harassed her ten years prior to his 1991 nomination, had a flimsy story—yet the same feminists who rushed to Hill's cause turned their backs when Paula Jones, Juanita Broaddrick, and Kathleen Willey accused President Bill Clinton of inappropriate sexual behavior in the workplace.
Photograph by Brad Markel/Liaison/ Getty Images)

Radical feminist Andrea Dworkin's declaration that every man is a covert rapist repulsed me no less than the sadistic question that used to be asked of sexually assaulted women: Did you enjoy it? *(Photograph by William Foley/Time Life Pictures/ Getty Images)*

When suicide pilots destroyed the World Trade Center, feminist and sixties radical Barbara Ehrenreich admitted she found it "heartbreaking" that the September 11 perpetrators subscribed to "such a violent and misogynist ideology." If only the pilots believed in taking their daughters to work! *(Photograph by Fred LeBlanc)*

considered myself pro-choice but rethought the abortion
ssue when several Senate Democrats blithely insisted that the
arbaric practice of partial-birth abortion is a morally neutral
choice."

Photograph by Tim Boyle/Getty Images)

Princeton ethics professor and animal-rights zealot Peter
Singer said he "would rather brush away an insect than kill it"
but declared it ethically okay to kill one-year-old children
with physical or mental disabilities, as well as Alzheimer's
patients, because the condition makes them "non-persons."
(Photograph by Frank Jacobs/Times of Trenton)

Any inclination to consider Noam Chomsky a legitimate voice of protest disappeared for me when, with the rubble of the twin towers still smoking, the MIT professor rushed to blame America for September 11, blithely declaring that the death toll was minor compared with Third World victims of the "far more extreme terrorism" of United States foreign policy.
(Photograph by Sebastian Willnow/AFP/Getty Images)

Ted Kennedy's shameless willingness to compare isolated prisoner abuse at Abu Ghraib prison with Saddam's nationwide system of torture chambers marked a new low even for Kennedy, who had earlier called the Iraq war "a fraud made up in Texas to give Republicans a political boost" (even though Kennedy had previously declared that Saddam's "pursuit of lethal weapons of mass destruction cannot be tolerated"). *(Photograph by Mike Theiler/Getty Images)*

After propagandizing on behalf of the North Vietnamese government, insisting that American POWs were being treated humanely, and calling them "war criminals," then denouncing them as liars for claiming they had been tortured, Jane Fonda three decades later had the audacity to declare herself the real victim: "I was framed and turned into a lightning rod for people's anger." Naturally she also blamed "patriarchy" for making her get breast implants and for her decision to recruit women to join her in sexual romps with husband Roger Vadim.
(Photograph by Jorge Uzon/AFP/Getty Images)

With American troops in harm's way, it was stomach turning to hear Michael Moore take the side of the beheaders of Baghdad when he declared, "The Iraqis who have risen up against the occupation are not 'insurgents' or 'terrorists' or 'The Enemy.' They are the REVOLUTION, the Minutemen, and their numbers will grow—and they will win."
(Photograph by Kevin Winter/Getty Images)

Demonstrators burned a U.S. flag in protest against the war in Iraq on October 25, 2003, in Washington, D.C., amid signs demanding an end to the war, racism, and ethnic scapegoating. No one reported hearing protesters' objecting to suicide pilots or Saddam's mass graves. *Photograph by Jeff Fusco/Getty Images)*

Warning: Testimony may contain explicit details. CNN

Having celebrated the uncovering of Nixon's Watergate evasions and high crimes, I found it appalling to hear Democrats proclaim that Clinton's obstruction of justice and perjury didn't count because the subject matter was "only" sex.
(AFP/AFP/Getty Images)

Clinton defender James Carville showed the administration's shallow commitment to women's issues when he contemptuously dismissed Paula Jones's sexual harassment claim against Clinton. "Drag a hundred-dollar bill through a trailer park and there's no telling what you'll get."
(Photograph by Nicholas Kamm/AFP/ Getty Images)

until just now, whereupon there follows a treatise about how important it is to listen to others, which usually runs something like this: People who, like me, engage in caring dialogue, which is free of domination and attack, have found a new way to meet each other, not on the pattern of discourse as a war to be won, but as a show of how caring and loving we really are, and you can see how caring and loving we really are by comparing us to all those people who do not follow our example (whereupon there usually ensues a list of the uncaring culprit's wicked ways, which just happens to have the advantage, not really intended, of making the lecturer's moral superiority blindingly obvious to the entire world).

In this very spirit, Clinton's defenders became extraordinarily adept at claiming to inhabit a higher moral ground, even as they heaped contempt on the investigators pursuing clear evidence of attempts to violate the law and undermine constitutional government. Check this for higher ground: Harvard philosopher Michael J. Sandal wrote that "there may be a case, in the name of privacy and decorum, for the president to deny a scurrilous charge even if true, provided it has no bearing on public responsibilities." As for heaping contempt, James Carville took obvious delight in scorning Kenneth Starr's habit of singing hymns on morning walks along the Potomac River: "He plants a story, he goes down by the Potomac and listens to hymns, as the cleansing waters of the Potomac go by, and we are going to wash all the Sodomites and fornicators out of town."

So it went throughout the first half of 1998. Clinton defenders spoke for worldwise sophistication of a distinctly European type; Clinton's critics stood for blue-nosed Puritanism and refused to respect the president's right to privacy.

Cultural analyses aside, here is what matters. The president of the United States lied under oath. The extent to which some of his defenders sought to explain this away was at times mind-boggling. Appearing on the Fox News program *Hannity & Colmes,* Democratic strategist Vic Kamber went beyond simply parroting the White House talking points for that particular day. Kamber insisted that Clinton and Lewinsky had never engaged in sexual activity, even though the physical evidence—including Lewinsky's own forthcoming testimony—was already in and irrefutable.

"If there is semen on the dress," Vic insisted (with a straight face), "it still may not be a sexual relationship as defined by the agreement with the judge."

Kamber was referring to a tortuous definition of sex insisted upon by Clinton's defense team, in which Clinton could say—as he said under oath—that he had not had sexual relations with Lewinsky because (get ready) he did not touch her genitals, breast, or thigh as she favored him with oral sex.

As key moderate voters joined the derisive laughter of conservatives, team Clinton attempted to shift its defense away from any justification of what happened between Bill and Monica to an expanded definition of character that meshed nicely with the baby boomers' sense of themselves as saving the world. Presidential apologists took to the airwaves to insist that the true test of Clinton's presidency is how we are doing on crucial and complex issues like health care, education, welfare, and the environment. House minority leader Dick Gephardt groused about "the time that this [Starr investigation] has taken," since it steals the nation's attention "away from the things that we most should be working on—education, health care, pensions, jobs, wages, the economy, moving the country in the right direction."

Radcliffe College fellow Wendy Kaminer insisted that "there is something childlike and potentially dangerous about expecting the president to serve as our moral exemplar; that's what monks and demagogues do." Many Americans would have been happy simply to see the president behave like a grown-up, or at least meet his constitutional responsibility to "take care that the laws be faithfully executed." In 1974 I cheered when Texas representative Barbara Jordan made it clear that she took her role altogether seriously as an investigator of crimes against the law of the land:

> Today I am an inquisitor. An hyperbole would not be fictional and would not overstate the solemnness that I feel right now. My faith in the Constitution is whole; it is complete; it is total. And I am not going to sit here and be an idle spectator to the diminution, the subversion, the destruction, of the Constitution.

In fairness, not every Democrat drank the Clinton Kool-Aid. A few brave souls weathered the contempt of their partisan colleagues by making it clear that they found the president's actions reprehensible and demanding that he be held to account. I wanted to give Senator Joseph Lieberman a huge high five for refusing to defend the indefensible when he spoke to the U.S. Senate on September 3, 1998:

> To begin with, I must respectfully disagree with the President's contention that his relationship with Monica Lewinsky and the way in which he misled us about it is "nobody's business but" his family's and that "even presidents have private lives," as he said. Whether he or we as a people think it fair or not, the reality in 1998 is that a president's private life is public. Contemporary news media standards will have it no other way. Surely this President was given fair warning of that by the amount of time the news media has dedicated to

investigating his personal life during the 1992 campaign and in the years since.

But there is more to this than modern media intrusiveness. The President is not just the elected leader of our country, he is, as presidential scholar Clinton Rossiter observed, "the one-man distillation of the American people," and "the personal embodiment and representative of their dignity and majesty," as President Taft once said. So when his personal conduct is embarrassing, it is so not just for him and his family. It is embarrassing for us all as Americans.

The President is also a role model, who, because of his prominence and the moral authority that emanates from his office, sets standards of behavior for the people he serves. . . . So no matter how much the President or others may wish to "compartmentalize" the different spheres of his life, the inescapable truth is that the President's private conduct can and often does have profound public consequences.

In this case, the President apparently had extramarital relations with an employee half his age, and did so in the workplace, in the vicinity of the Oval Office. Such behavior is not just inappropriate. It is immoral. And it is harmful, for it sends a message of what is acceptable behavior to the larger American family, particularly to our children, which is as influential as the negative messages communicated by the entertainment culture. If you doubt that, just ask America's parents about the intimate and often unseemly sexual questions their young children have been asking and discussing since the President's relationship with Ms. Lewinsky became public seven months ago.

I have had many of those conversations in recent

days, and from that I can conclude that many parents feel much as I do, that something very sad and sordid has happened in American life when I cannot watch the news on television with my ten-year-old daughter any more.

Lieberman's declaration of conscience marked yet another turning point; suddenly it was impossible for all but the most extreme Clinton defenders to continue denying the relevance of Clinton's moral lapse to his capacity to govern with credibility. Hoping to regain the home court advantage, team Clinton returned to its earlier emphasis on the *technical* nature of the president's violations—or as it hoped to convey, Clinton's mere infractions. Hillary Clinton led the way by declaring, "We know very few facts." Former White House special counsel Lanny Davis elaborated: "There are facts, and there are nonfacts. At the moment we are looking at a bunch of allegations, unsubstantiated innuendo that has caused Ken Starr, I think, to misuse the subpoena power." Feeling the wind at his back for a change, Davis struck a confident tone: "Let's remember what this investigation is all about. It's about an alleged false statement in the middle of a civil case, which has been thrown out of court."

During the height of Watergate, imagine a diehard supporter of Richard Nixon taking to the airwaves and declaring, "Given that the special prosecutor Leon Jaworski is hell-bent on destroying him . . . it would be foolhardy for [the president] to cooperate in any way." Change Jaworski to Starr, and the rest of that quote is Lanny Davis warning about the danger Ken Starr posed to Bill Clinton, who, like King Lear, still viewed himself more sinned against than sinning. James Carville hammered the theme of Starr as out of control and perhaps deranged. "If there is a privilege that [President Clinton] can assert under the law, given the behavior of Mr. Starr and his henchmen, then he ought to assert that privilege, and clearly executive privilege and the attorney-client privilege. If there's a Fifth Amendment right the president can assert, I think he ought to assert that, because these people have gone around and subpoenaed mothers, they've subpoenaed bookstores, they've subpoenaed people to talk about conversations with reporters."

While Carville catches his breath, let's simply note that there was always a very different way Bill Clinton could have called Ken Starr's bluff. The president could have cooperated with the prosecutors, in a manner consistent with his protestations of innocence and his constitutional rights to due process. The president could have chosen to give a complete and full accounting of his actions. Clinton disingenuously insisted he wanted to do exactly that but was forbidden because he was "honoring the rules of the investigation." That's the ticket, Hillary apparently decided. "Because there's an investigation going on, nobody can expect the president to say anything more publicly, because if there weren't an investigation he could, but because there is an investigation, he can't."

For me the decisive moment had already come and gone. I turned in my symbolic credentials and abandoned team Clinton when, in response to Paula Jones's charge that President Clinton had sexually assaulted her, James Carville declared, "Drag a hundred-dollar bill through a trailer park, you never know what you'll find." Eventually Clinton paid Jones (whose plight had been ignored by the same feminist establishment that had gone after Senator Bob Packwood with torches and pitchforks when he was accused of sexually harassing his employees) an out-of-court settlement of $850,000.

All in all, during the crisis that threatened his presidency Bill Clinton said as little as he could, as much as he had to, when he had to, and only then. His press spokesman, Mike McCurry, was asked whether he wanted to know the truth behind the charges. "God, no. No, I don't really want to know." He added: "Knowing the truth means you have to tell the truth." (For heaven's sake, Mike, don't be so *literal*.)

Politically, we know how this story came out. On December 11 and 12, 1998, the House of Representatives voted to impeach the president. The Senate subsequently voted to acquit. Following the Senate vote, these were the president's words: "I want to say again to the American people how profoundly sorry I am for what I said and did to trigger these events and the great burden they have imposed on the Congress and on the American people." As usual, here's how Clinton's words came across: *I didn't do it. I wasn't even there. My political enemies are to blame. I'm done with this. It's irrelevant.*

Professor Hadley Arkes of Amherst College likes to tell the old joke about the lawyer who is promised unbounded success in business and love, but only at the price of giving up his soul at the end. And he asks, "What's the catch?"

According to Professor Arkes, "The accomplishment of Bill Clinton is that he made the country into one large lawyer joke. Clinton has marked off the record of an incorrigible liar, faithless to his wife, who cannot be trusted to honor law beyond his own interest, and the public says, 'Yes—but what is the problem?'"

I sense we're still collectively thinking that one through. If, as seems likely, Hillary runs for president, we'll find out whether we have the fortitude for another rendezvous with a couple who, like Tom and Daisy Buchanan in *The Great Gatsby*, have "always retreated back into their money or their vast carelessness, or whatever it was that kept them together, and let other people clean up the mess they had made." Just before the House impeachment vote David Schippers, chief counsel to the House impeachment effort, memorably declared, "There's no one left to lie to." Oh, really? Let's find out. On with the campaign!

CHAPTER SEVEN

COLUMBINE CALLING AMERICA

Pay Attention to Your Kids

The diary of a Columbine High School student discloses that he and another student gunman planned their bloody massacre at the school for more than a year, police said Saturday. . . . [The sheriff] noted that along with the diary, police found a shotgun barrel on a dresser of one of the boy's homes, as well as bomb-making materials. "A lot of this stuff was clearly visible and the parents should have known."

—CNN News, April 25, 1999

I had just put my four-month-old son down for a nap when I flicked on the TV, hoping to learn something interesting about life in the world beyond the front sidewalk. The breaking news from the town of Littleton, Colorado, was grim. Two students wearing black trench coats, Eric Harris, eighteen, and Dylan Klebold, seventeen, had laughed and hooted as they opened fire on classmates in their suburban Denver high school, killing fifteen people, including themselves, in America's worst instance of school violence. The day was April 20, 1999.

If you are a parent, I can only imagine your reaction to the slaughter at Columbine High School was like mine. You must have felt dread. No matter where you live, you must have felt like Littleton was just a few miles down the road. You probably thought about your own kids' daily schedules. Were they OK that very day? Maybe you drove to school early and peered through their classroom windows. I checked in on my sleeping son that afternoon a few times more than usual.

And perhaps also like me, you stayed tuned in in hopes of hearing something that made sense amid all the usual responses from all the usual talking heads. Ten days after the shooting, Susan Bitter Smith wrote a heartfelt essay in the *Arizona Republic*. Three compelling paragraphs stood out:

> Many pundits on air and in print have pontificated on the reasons for the tragedy and offered solutions. Many politicians have used the tragedy as a platform to push for their favorite social reforms.
>
> This isn't about new penalties, gun control, or Internet censorship.
>
> It's about attention, involvement, and attitude.

Attention: noticing weapons and hate propaganda left in plain view in the Columbine shooters' bedrooms. Involvement: asking questions about videos produced for class projects with themes like murdering members of the school's sports teams. Attitude: being willing to violate that most fundamental sixties-era commandment, "Thou shalt not be judgmental." Don't look now, but that's a *judgment against judging*. Tell the truth: Doesn't it feel *good* to recognize the self-canceling character of the demand not to hold judgments? Doesn't it seem sort of grown up to take a deep breath and affirm, "I don't have to justify why I want to read the lyric sheets in my kids' CDs; why I do periodic, unannounced checks of the Web sites their computers visit; why I ask where they've been, where they're headed in such a hurry, who they'll be with, and what kinds of ideas are printed in their school text-books."

I have had that experience a lot since becoming a parent. After some initial resistance I think I'm getting used to it. Actually it's satisfying.

Like many members of the baby-boom generation, easily the most self-centered in American history, I extended my adolescence as long as possible. The parents of the Columbine students are part of my generation, and we were different, and special, and most assuredly wiser than our parents, whose generational authority was intrinsically suspect. Never trust anyone older than thirty, declared the sixties. How did this morph into a belief that as a parent you had no right to notice armaments in your kid's bedroom? Let's thank the "counterculture."

Social critic Theodore Roszak popularized that phrase in a 1969 book called *The Making of a Counter Culture*. Roszak called for elevating and celebrating each individual's personal construction of reality and their lashing out against the prevailing rational, conventional, objective standards represented by the 1950s. To be truly counterculture today means recognizing the disastrous social and cultural effects of that movement, most especially a rampant narcissism that hides behind platitudes like:

> What's true for you is not necessarily true for me, though thanks for sharing. What's right is simply what particular individuals or cultures happen to agree on at any given moment, so go for it. Each person is free to find his or her own values, so long as they're not binding on anybody else. I do my thing, you do yours. Maybe we'll connect along the way, maybe not. Keep it real, dude.

You may not talk that way, you may not believe you think that way, and your birth certificate might prove you're not part of the baby-boom generation (born between 1946 and 1964). Even so, the values underlying those pop-psych platitudes are part of your world in the sense conveyed by the ancient Chinese aphorism: A fish is the last one to know it lives in water. Those values are very much at the heart of the contemporary left's counterculture agenda: an anything-goes pluralism, a radical moral relativism, a social construction of reality, an unrelenting opposition to any form of hierarchy, an immersion in subjectivity, and paranoia about making any judgments that might "marginalize" some individual or group: *If my kids want to wear black trench coats and ghoulish makeup and black nail polish, shouldn't I honor that? I don't want to damage their self-esteem.*

Once upon a time—roughly prior to 1956—raising kids seemed fairly simple, which is to say straightforward, meaning child rearing was the subject of not much thought and even less talk. A parent was something you were, not something you *did*; the noun *parenting* (it didn't exist) would have drawn the blankest of stares. It was a time, says poet and culture sage Robert Bly, when kids "in grade school knew to sit down, to behave, to repress sexual impulses, to hold their bodies stiffly, to salute the flag and stand up when a teacher enters the room."

Social critic Michael Ventura says this all changed in a single moment in 1956, when Elvis Presley gyrated his pelvis to music on national television. "All the parents in the United States lost their children in a single night," Ventura writes. By the end of the 1960s, a new generation was no longer willing to live "by fear, by internalized superintendents, by shaming, by workaholism," Bly continues. "It felt as if human beings were able for the first time in history to choose their own roads, choose what to do with their bodies, choose the visionary possibilities formerly shut off by that 'control system.' "

As liberation movements proliferated during the 1960s and 1970s, children joined the growing ranks of America's oppressed, put there by advocates who asserted that children were little people who had been deprived of a voice in their own destiny. In this view the child deserved equal standing in the social world; adult rules and boundaries were unnecessary infringements on the child's liberty. Extreme, perhaps, but an idea that's become sufficiently diffused into the culture of parenthood so that all too many parents no longer feel free to tell a child what to do. Instead, they engage in what one writer calls a "tot-level Socratic dialogue" that starts with the abnegation of parental authority, whether about when the child should go to bed or whether he or she would go to school on any given day. "All right, you tell me what you think you should do," a parent now asks, praying that the child will come up with the "right" answer.

A northern California mother named Ellie and a father named Frank, who had both seen Elvis Presley gyrate on TV four decades earlier, ruefully describe what Ellie calls their "utterly bizarre" response to learning that their teenage daughter, Susan, had stopped attending French class. "Her teacher called and asked Frank and me to get on the phone together," Ellie recalls. "I was floored when I learned that Susan had just dropped out. My immediate silent reaction was that Susan would have to return to class. [But] with that thought came a sharp twinge of guilt. I felt I was somehow betraying my daughter. When I finally spoke into the phone, I heard myself say something about how her father and I had tried to raise Susan to make her own decisions."

"My own gut response was the same," says Frank. "Susan needs to know it's important in life to finish what you start. But something kept me from forming those words. I declared myself in agreement with Ellie—Susan needed to decide for herself. The most amazing thing was the lack of anger or urgency in our voices. It was like we both didn't feel we had the right to tell our adolescent daughter that we expected her to get an education."

Ellie and Frank aren't alone, says Oakland psychologist Diane

Ehrensaft, author of *Spoiling Childhood: How Well-Meaning Parents Are Giving Children Too Much—But Not What They Need.*

The baby boomers are a generation of self-involved, self-indulgent parents, who go to extremes in pursuit of our personal happiness and professional fulfillment. But we are also a generation with a tremendous commitment to being good parents, who often go overboard in providing what we think will be the best for our children. This is the lethal combination that puts so many of us at risk for spoiling childhood.

Ehrensaft believes several factors are simultaneously at work. In previous decades there were dominant directives about raising children—for instance, the 1930s advocacy of early habit training. These days parents typically find themselves frantically hopping from one child-rearing approach to another—democratic to autocratic, permissive to authoritative, indulgent to withholding. Furthermore, parents are stretched not only between family and work but between changing assumptions about parental roles. Mom is expected to be in the workplace, but also at home; Dad is supposed to achieve mightily at work, and also be a caring father. "The structure of the workplace; the changes in family life; the increasing unpredictability of the environmental, social, and political world; and the sensibilities of a society that puts profit first and families last all have had a deep psychological effect on the men and women who conceive and raise children today," Ehrensaft says.

All crucial elements, yet none of them quite gets to why or how Ellie and Frank came to think of adult limits and boundaries as unnecessary infringements on their daughter's sovereignty.

Harvard psychologist Dan Kindlon traces many of today's parenting woes to the marked ambivalence that took root in the 1960s spirit of protest. "Our generation came up with the bumper sticker 'Question Authority,'" Kindlon writes in his book *Too Much of a Good Thing: Raising Children of Character in an Indulgent Age.*

> Having grown up under the influence of Vietnam, Watergate, and other cultural cataclysms of the '60s and '70s, many parents today are more distrustful of authority than their parents were and as a result they are less comfortable wielding power over their children, including setting strict limits. You can clean your child's room in 10 minutes, but it may take you a half an hour of struggle to have them clean it themselves. Guess who usually cleans the room?

Kindlon believes boomer parents are more likely than previous generations to depend on their children to give meaning to their lives.

> It's kind of a childhood-as-Prozac phenomenon. We use our children's happiness to make us happy, so we are reluctant to be strict about their behavior in ways that would upset them or jeopardize our relationships with them. And because families tend to be smaller now, each child becomes that much more precious. We want to protect our children from all kinds of pain; we hope they'll have perfect lives, devoid of hardship and pain. But their happiness as adults is largely dependent on the tools we give them, tools that will allow them to develop emotional maturity, to be honest with themselves, to be empathetic, to take initiative, to delay gratification, to learn from failure and move on, to accept their flaws, and to face the consequences when they've done something wrong.

Kay Hymowitz, author of *Liberation's Children: Parents and Kids in a Postmodern Age,* emphatically shares Kindlon's concern. "The same forces that have liberated today's kids from want, settled life paths, and confining traditions have also 'freed' them from the moral and spiritual guidance that has always come from parents, teachers, and the culture at large," Hymowitz says.

The result is not that today's kids 'have no values,' as pundits often tell us. On the contrary: American children develop Victorian-size superegos dedicated to the command to realize themselves through work. They hear endless moralizing about the virtues of tolerance and open-mindedness. The problem is that these virtues, important as they are, cannot help the young person build a self. Unmoored from all inherited structures of meaning, they tell kids not to judge, but not what to believe. They tell them to embrace all, but not what matters. They tell them to choose, but not why or how. In short, liberation's children live in a culture that frees the mind and soul by emptying them.

Eager to understand how indulgence, affluence, and character development are related, Kindlon conducted a study of well-to-do adolescents. He was interested not only in headline problems like substance abuse and eating disorders but also in emotional problems, including depression and anxiety. He and his research assistants gave questionnaires to 650 teenagers, asking them things such as, are they happy? do they get along with their parents? do they drink or take drugs?

The researchers also asked what kinds of things the kids owned—for instance, do they have their own cell phone or a car? and how much allowance do they get? Kindlon was especially curious about what was required of the teenagers by their parents.

Were their parents strict about having them keep their rooms clean, or helping with the dishes? Do they have a curfew? A similar survey went to more than a thousand parents, with questions asking whether they think their children are happy, did they buy them a cell phone, and how strict they are. This sample included not only parents of teenagers but also parents of younger children.

Approximately 40 percent of the teenagers Kindlon studied described themselves as seriously depressed, but when researchers asked the parents if they thought their child was depressed, very few thought they were. As for anxiety, about one of every four teenagers was classified as "very worried." Around 60 percent of the kids had used tobacco, alcohol, or illegal drugs during the past month. One in four had very permissive attitudes toward premarital sex. The majority of parents—around 60 percent—stated that their child is spoiled, and a significant number of their children agreed with them. Moreover, a near majority of parents also acknowledged that they are less strict than their parents were. "About 12 percent of the kids didn't have any of the problems we studied," Kindlon notes. "There were four factors that distinguished them from everyone else. Their families frequently ate dinner together, their parents weren't divorced, they weren't allowed to have a phone in their room, and they regularly did community service."

Robert Bly believes we're fast becoming a nation of siblings. "In many ways, we are now living in a culture run by half-adults," he writes in *The Sibling Society*. He argues that Elvis signaled the beginning of a long overdue shift from a paternal society dominated by "the bald, the severe, the cabined, the icebound, the squat, the cramped, the dinky, the narrow, the scanty, the roped-in, the meager, the bad, the tame." By the late 1960s, he says, "the superego took its hands away from the throats of young people, or so it seemed, and the whole nation relaxed, felt less depression, endured less repression. The Beatles said something, happily, about living in a yellow submarine."

But things went too far. Today we're fast becoming a culture of siblings in which impulse is given its way at every turn. In such a society, "it is hard to know how to approach one's children, what values to try to teach them, what to stand up for, what to go along with; it is especially hard to know where your children are."

"So many parents are so lost. They don't know what to or how to. They are so stretched. Caught by the choices they have made." Elise Webster is musing about the changes she's seen in parenting over the many years she's been working to "show kids they have everything it takes to save the world, and the world needs them more than ever." That sounds grandiose, but it is actually her simple way of describing how she conveys to the preschool children she teaches that they are "welcome and worthy."

"What I try to communicate is my expectation that they can make a tremendous difference," says Webster, director of the Children's Cultural Center of Marin, just north of San Francisco.

I convey my absolute certainty, no question about it. Last week, there was a ten-pound bag of carrots that needed moving. I asked a fifteen-month-old boy to carry the carrots over to the refrigerator. He dragged it and loved doing it and felt enormous satisfaction, looking around for what else needed doing. The word 'chore' never got mentioned. Kids love to contribute. They're never too young to contribute in the household, to put a place mat on, laundry in the machine.

Webster says she sees

a deep sorrow, something so missing in the family dynamics in our culture now. It's a vicious circle. Time is at a premium. But I believe parents would create more time, if they found more pleasure in their family lives. The key is expecting appropriate behavior from the very beginning, and reinforcing for respect. To build in a child a sense of team early is critical. Kids need to know they are part of the tapestry of life, and they are needed and necessary and appreciated.

Bonnie Romanow smiles when a parent asks which is more important in raising a child: love or discipline? She likes this question, because it gives her a chance to answer "yes." She doesn't accept the premise that genuine discipline and authentic love are somehow at odds, or even fundamentally different.

"The word *discipline* is derived from the Latin word *disciple*," says Romanow, parent education coordinator of Parents Place, a division of Jewish Family and Children's Services in Santa Rosa, California. "And to be a disciple is to follow a person or activity out of admiration and love, with a desire to learn from and emulate. We know how open and accepting children are. What our kids need more than anything else is an unmistakable and ongoing sense of engaged presence."

Romanow says she respects the impulse of so many parents to see that all parts of their children's lives are taken care of. The paradox is that doing this successfully requires knowing when not to do something for one's child, which in turn means learning to be a skilled observer of subtle aspects of your kid's behavior.

"Think about two different ways to structure an infant's relationship with a rattle," Romanow suggests.

On the one hand, you can choose to always place the rattle within the baby's reach. Over time, this teaches infants that what they want will always be within their immediate grasp, which can lead them to believe that parents—or someone parentlike—will always be there to help out. On the other hand, you can put the rattle just beyond the infant's reach. This gives babies practice in stretching, extending themselves both physically and psychologically. But this can be difficult for parents, because babies make distress sounds that often cause parents to come to the rescue.

She emphasizes, of course, that assisting is not always bad and adversity is not always good. "The real goal is to develop and trust your capacity to tune in to your child's authentic needs, and your child's capacity for autonomy in life-affirming relationships with others." An important key is balance, says Romanow, a former Waldorf preschool teacher who found her own experience as a young mother with two little girls echoed in the isolation, confusion, and uncertainty experienced by many parents.

"Balance in our lives rarely means exactly fifty-fifty. What works and what is needed changes over time as our family unit grows and changes." In her private practice Romanow frequently finds herself encouraging parents of young children, saying that it's OK to stand as an authority to their children. "Our own fears of being too controlling, like our parents, or squelching our child's sense of individuality can prevent us from providing the structure and boundaries a child needs to feel safe and confident," she says. "Naturally, we want our children to be free, but freedom is a heavy burden for a young child. Your child wants you to be firm and certain, which in the final analysis is not different from a loving sense of inner rightness and a spirit of adventure that I call parenting from the heart."

Yet inner rightness is precisely the factor that so often proves vexing for baby-boom parents, who have a hard time sorting out their own needs from those of their kids. Such parents "vacillate wildly between catering to their children as the center of the universe," says Diane Ehrensaft, "and seeing their sons and daughters only through the lens of their own needs." An issue of *People,* for instance, reported breathlessly on two recent midlife mothers, Geena Davis and Julianne Moore, whose achievements in giving birth were described in terms suggesting that these two actors are big-time role models for the rest of us—simply by existing.

"She never had one problem during her pregnancy, not one bit of morning sickness," gushes Bill Davis, Geena's dad. "And Geena said the birth was no big deal. She was in labor something like four-and-a-half hours. For a first-time birth, and at her age, it's amazing. *She's* amazing." Speaking of absolutely fabulous, Julianne Moore ranks pretty darned close to the top herself. "Juli says having babies gets addictive because it's so exciting," says her boyfriend and the father of her two-week-old daughter, Liv. "Age isn't an issue for her."

Giving birth in your midforties is a notable physical accomplishment. And, to be fair, these characterizations of the birth process are secondhand, attributed to the two mothers by men who are understandably thrilled. Still, it's hard not to scratch your head at the unabashed narcissism of the *People* accounts. Who knows? Maybe Davis and Moore will be exceptional parents. At the very least, it would be interesting to hear their answers, a year from now, to the deceptively simple question Diane Ehrensaft asks of boomer parents in *Spoiling Childhood:* "Who am I doing this for, me or my child?" It would be equally interesting to hear how the new dads handle the same question—given the precious subheading of a 1996 *Parenting* magazine article: "A father searches for himself in his newborn's face."

Near the end of *The Sibling Society* Robert Bly gives a stirring vision of the larger challenge our culture faces, at the frontier between generations:

What is asked of adults now is that they . . . turn to face the young siblings and the adolescents. One can imagine a field with the adolescents on one side of a line drawn on the earth and adults on the other side looking into their eyes. The adult in our time is asked to reach his or her hand across the line and pull the youth into adulthood. That means of course that the adults will have to decide what genuine adulthood is. If the adults do not turn and walk up to this line and help pull the adolescents over, the adolescents will stay exactly where they are for another twenty or thirty years. If we don't turn to face the young ones, their detachment machines, which are louder and more persistent than ours, will say, "I am not part of this family," and they will kill any real relationship with their parents. The parents have to know that.

No small task—but first things first. Boomer parents (along with Gen X and Y parents, who aren't immune from the culture's larger currents) need to look their children in the eye, then look in the mirror, and come away absolutely clear who's the kid here. Everything important will follow from that.

CHAPTER EIGHT

BLAMING AMERICA FIRST
The Left Goes Berserk on 9/11

[The September 11 suicide pilots] were targeting those people I referred to as "little Eichmanns." These were legitimate targets.

—Ward Churchill, University of Colorado professor

When the notorious vehicles of death assaulted the World Trade Center and the Pentagon on September 11, 2001, American leftists found themselves standing on strange and uncertain ground—but in a way that differed substantially from the experience of most Americans that day. Most of us didn't blame America for the pilots' murderous acts.

In the aftermath of Vietnam, self-styled progressives got used to automatically assuming the worst about U.S. foreign policy, defining themselves as permanent dissenters from a cultural center they loved to hate. Charmed for decades by Third World revolutionaries mouthing pious clichés against the accumulated evils of the West, the left faced in Osama bin Laden an enemy who shared their chronic contempt for the United States but made "no pretense at any universal, secular ideology that could appeal to Western liberals," as Andrew Sullivan wrote at the time.

This was new terrain for America's self-willed exiles in residence—but not exactly a deal breaker. Just because bin Laden didn't inspire feelings of solidarity among reflexive critics of America's global presence was hardly a reason to lose sight of the true culprit—America herself. The acknowledged master of this genre is an embittered East Coast academic who remains unknown to most Americans because his goal is to inculcate into fringe, dissident intellectuals his central article of faith that America is a threat to the survival of the world. After four decades of intense political activism, MIT professor Noam Chomsky has attained the status of a left-wing cult figure ("the L. Ron Hubbard of the New Left," one writer called him) for giving voice to the visceral hatred of America that has been an enduring fact of our national life since the 1960s.

An unapologetic proponent of Hanoi during the U.S. engagement in Vietnam, Chomsky surpassed his America-bashing compatriots Jane Fonda and Tom Hayden by continuing to serve the Vietnamese revolution after Hanoi, in the name of "reeducation," sentenced hundreds of thousands of Vietnamese to Hanoi's gulag, and forced tens of thousands of "boat people" to flee for their lives and perish on the open seas. Confronted with evidence of these homicidal policies, Chomsky had only two questions: Whose interests were served by these unhelpful reports? and, how could the reports be refuted?

Given his intense suspicion toward everything America does in the world, his scrutiny of the American media and his belief that his fellow citizens are the victims of "manufactured consent" that renders them citizens in name only, Chomsky has demonstrated remarkably little interest in the lack of free speech in his beloved Communist Vietnam. In his book *At War with Asia* Chomsky waxes positively radiant about his visits there in 1970. He called the South Vietnamese regime "authoritarian and repressive" but neglected to mention the North Vietnamese government's slaughter of three thousand civilians two years earlier in Hue, an event about which he was already well informed.

In 1970, Chomsky gave a speech in North Vietnam, praising the nation as a worker's paradise. "We saw luxurious fields and lovely countryside. We saw brave men and women who know how to defend their country from brutal aggression, but also to work with pride and with dignity to build a society of material prosperity, social justice, and cultural progress. I would like to express the great joy that we feel in your accomplishments." Then he denounced the United States. "In the midst of the creative achievements of the Vietnamese people, we came face-to-face with the savagery of a technological monster controlled by a social class, the rulers of the American empire, that has no place in the twentieth century, that has only the capacity to repress and murder and destroy." He offered his hope that Vietnam was moving "toward the socialist society in which free, creative men control their own destiny. . . . Decent people throughout the world see in your struggle a model for themselves."

When American troops left southeast Asia, Chomsky directed his animosity at witnesses and reporters who testified to the massive human catastrophe of the Cambodian genocide that took place in the aftermath of the Communist victory and American withdrawal. At first Chomsky tried to play down the deaths (a "few thousand") when there was growing evidence that the deaths numbered in the hundreds of thousands. He compared those killed by Pol Pot and his cohorts to the collaborators who died at the hands of resistance movements in Europe after World War II. By 1980 the world had become aware that some 2 million of Cambodia's 7.8 million people had perished at the hands of the Pol Pot regime. Continuing to deny the reality of a systematic killing campaign, Chomsky blamed the deaths on a failure of the rice crop. When photographs of skulls piling up became widely available, Chomsky returned to his all-purpose explanation: The United States was to blame for whatever happened in Cambodia.

In October 2003 Chomsky paid a visit to Cuba, and was greeted warmly by Vice President Ricardo Alarcon. "It is the first time Noam Chomsky is in Cuba," he said, "but Cuba has always been in him." During the Reagan era, Chomsky argued that the quality of life in Cuba was equal to that in the United States. Later he bumped up his estimate, saying Cuba is "actually better than the United States if we consider its more egalitarian character, thus with lower infant mortality rates than Chicago and far lower rates than the Navajo reservation." During his 2003 visit, speaking before an audience that included Fidel Castro, Chomsky made an appearance on state-owned Radio Havana. Amazingly, this champion of free speech passed up an opportunity to speak up for Cuban political dissidents, including the thousands of political prisoners being held in Castro's gulag. But Chomsky didn't pass up a chance to stand up for those jailed in the United States. Imprisoned on charges of spying, Chomsky declared them "five patriotic Cuban prisoners."

In light of this background it is not surprising that in his first statement about Osama bin Laden's premeditated assaults on office buildings containing thousands of innocent civilians, Chomsky could not resist minimizing the crime compared with an even greater atrocity the victim had committed:

> The terrorist attacks were major atrocities. In scale they may not reach the level of many others; for example, Clinton's bombing of the Sudan with no credible pretext, destroying half its pharmaceutical supplies and killing unknown numbers of people (no one knows, because the U.S. blocked an inquiry at the UN and no one cares to pursue it).

This is pure Chomsky: his reference to the actual attacks little more than a curt preliminary to a standard pronouncement that America is to blame. In point of fact, Bill Clinton's decision to launch a missile into Sudan bore no parallel to the World Trade Center carnage. However poorly executed, the missile attack was launched in response to the blowing up of two U.S. embassies in Africa by Islamic terrorists, resulting in the murder of hundreds of innocent people and injury to thousands. Clinton's attack was designed to minimize the loss of innocent life, whereas the terrorists acting against the African embassies, the Pentagon, and the World Trade Center aimed to maximize the slaughter of innocents.

Chomsky wasn't alone in attacking his country. "What has the United States done to make itself this kind of target?" America is "an imperialist nation who exploits, starves, and kills civilians around the world—daily." "This is a case of the chickens coming home to roost." These statements were uttered on college campuses in Boulder, Madison, and Morgantown. Of the September 11 carnage, a Rutgers professor summed up the consensus by informing her students that "we should be aware that, whatever its proximate cause, its ultimate cause is the fascism of U.S. foreign policy over the past many decades." At Marquette University anti-American demonstrators blocked undergraduates from holding a moment of silence around the flag. Residence hall directors in Central Michigan University's Emmons dormitory combed the halls in search of doors adorned with forbidden patriotic images and statements. Don Pasco, a sophomore who had pictures of an American eagle and the World Trade Center taken off his door, said, "It was the whole hall. American flags or pictures that were pro-American had to be taken down because they were offending people."

Cafeteria supervisors at Arizona State University worried that an American flag hanging in plain view might offend foreign students, so they took it down. Florida Gulf Coast University's head librarian banned her staff from wearing "I'm proud to be an American" stickers in the days following the attacks. The librarian insisted, "We're doing everything we can to meet FGCU's standards of civility and tolerance." Margaret Post, a secretary in Holy Cross College's sociology department, lost a friend (Todd Beamer, believed to have helped foil the hijackers' suicide mission) on United flight 93 and wanted to honor him by hanging a flag outside her office. Furious professors called for its removal. Post refused, so department head Royce Singleton took it down himself. Singleton refused to explain his actions to the local media, saying only, "There is nothing I can say that will make anybody understand the social context in which this occurred."

Professors quickly joined the "blame America first" fray. "The *New York Times* headline was 'U.S. Attacked,'" historian Chalmers Johnson sneered. "That's insane. In many ways," he told a group at Yale, the terrorists "rightly identify us as the leader of those who are trying to keep them down." University of Massachusetts–Amherst journalism professor Bill Israel observed, "Many commentators are describing the disasters in New York as terrorist attacks—the worst since Pearl Harbor sixty years ago." Israel wasn't buying it. "None I've seen call them what they are: the predictable result of American policy." Professor Robert Jensen of the University of Texas–Austin announced that he directed his "primary anger at the leaders of this country" and insisted that the attacks on the Pentagon and the World Trade Center are "no more despicable than the massive acts of terrorism—the deliberate killing of civilians for political purposes—that the U.S. government has committed in my lifetime."

American University professor Peter Kuznick turned his history class into a seminar to blame the United States for the attacks, and insinuated that an American conspiracy was at work. "This is very convenient, the Pentagon needs an enemy, and now they have one—very convenient that such opportunistic things happen," said Kuznick, who teaches a course on Oliver Stone's cinematic view of history. University of New Mexico professor Richard Berthold bluntly informed his students, "Anyone who can blow up the Pentagon would get my vote." He repeated his assertion to his next class.

Military intervention to remove the Taliban would likely result in "a war that may destroy much of human society," Chomsky declared, casting doubt on the idea that Osama bin Laden had engineered the September 11 attacks. While acknowledging "the prima facie plausibility of the charge," he pronounced the evidence "surprisingly thin." Amazingly, Chomsky went on to declare: "Everyone was in favor of the overthrow of the Taliban, except the U.S. government."

If Chomsky was unambiguous in blaming America for the September 11 attacks, others on the "No War in My Name" left (translation: America is not entitled to defend itself) settled on a two-pronged policy: Exercise discipline by muzzling those hard-to-resist "America had it coming" sentiments, while staying on the lookout for opportunities to equate America's use of force in the world with the nihilistic mayhem of Islamist terror. The movement's first full-dress drill in moral equivalence came just after the White House and Congress resolved to strike at the heart of bin Laden's Afghanistan operations. Leading left intellectuals responded that when the number of civilians who died as a result of the war in Afghanistan exceeded the number of casualties caused by al Qaeda's September 11 mayhem, the Afghanistan war would be wrong, regardless of all other factors.

This masterwork of moral blindness neglected to ask two basic questions. What did the al Qaeda pilots intend to accomplish when they commandeered airplanes and crashed them into the Twin Towers? What did American soldiers intend to achieve when their actions resulted in the deaths of Afghani civilians? For those scoring at home, here are the correct answers. Al Qaeda sought to cause as many civilian deaths as possible. If they had been lucky, they might have been able to kill as many as fifty thousand people. No line was drawn between combatants and noncivilians; every individual in the World Trade Center was fair game. Had they the resources to take out all of Manhattan, they would have.

By contrast, American soldiers believed they were retaliating against the pilots' sponsors and accomplices. The soldiers intended to avoid civilian casualties, and took pains to do so. Premeditated murder versus unintended killing is the operative difference. This is a distinction that doesn't seem to compute in the bastions of the far left. Most Americans were clearly moved by the photos of Afghani women showing smiling faces to the world, of boys in shorts playing soccer, of men free to shave their beards, of girls finally allowed to attend school. Yet it was hard to avoid the impression that these images came as a slap in the face to the postcolonial left, with its shopworn theories of American imperialism and its reflex to side with Third World regimes against the accumulated evil of the West.

This is not to say that there was no sadness on the left after September 11—but it sounded closer to a kind of nostalgia, and again, how different from the experience of most Americans. Accustomed to arguing for the moral superiority of dictators like Fidel Castro, Daniel Ortega, and Ho Chi Minh, the American left seemed flummoxed that, at first blush, they didn't seem to share the same struggle with the latest camouflage-clad, olive-skinned anti-imperialist whose name was bin Laden.

An unmistakable lament filled Barbara Ehrenreich's confession in the *Village Voice:* "What is so heartbreaking to me as a feminist is that the strongest response to corporate globalization and U.S. military domination is based on such a violent and misogynist ideology." (If only the pilots had been pro-choice.) Fredric Jameson, a respected philosopher at Duke University, opined in the *London Review of Books* that the roots of the conflict could be traced to "the wholesale massacres of the Left systematically encouraged and directed by the Americans in an even earlier period. It is, however, only now that the results are working their way out into actuality, for the resultant absence of any Left alternative means that popular revolt and resistance in the Third World have nowhere to go but into religious and 'fundamentalist' forms."

Notice the quotation marks surrounding *fundamentalist,* by way of indicating that the speaker is not willing to concede the relevance of the adjective in describing bin Laden and company. In the far-left playbook of Chomsky and comrades, this new "terror thing" could only have its roots in global inequality and human poverty. Yes, the perpetrators do talk a lot about an "Islamic jihad against the infidel West," but this surely represents a kind of localized slang for the underlying common cause that unites all who rise up to strike the callous, cruel, rich, bullying, hedonistic, privileged, corrupt-beyond-remedy American empire. Critics like Jameson seemed to say: Let us look beyond their ceremonial religious trappings and understand that the wish list of the suicide pilots and their sponsors is at one with the aspirations of other idealistic (if somewhat misguided) anti-American revolutionaries: End the blockade of Iraq; get Starbucks out of Tierra del Fuego; establish a Palestinian state alongside Israel; withdraw American soldiers from everywhere (including Camp Pendleton). The secular left's contempt for the legitimacy of all forms of religious expression prevented them from recognizing how the theological component of Islamic fascism made it not just another group that attacks the imperial power in the name of the oppressed.

As usual, the interpretations of the anti-West left represented a projection of its own simmering disdain, which they have harbored for their country since the Vietnam era of the 1960s and 1970s. Against this backdrop, is it really difficult to understand why so few expressions of solidarity and empathy for the victims of September 11 were heard from bastions of the cultural left? Many who criticized the left's reflexive blame-America-first response missed a larger fact, hidden in plain view: Much of the cultural left may reside in the United States, but figuratively they don't really *live here* anymore. We know this because they say so every chance they get, and not only in the grandiose, adolescent bluster of the Chomsky contingent. In terms of kinship with the joys and sufferings of their fellow citizens, it is simply the case that a large portion of America's politically correct elite has not lived here for quite some time. The U.S. Census Department needs a new category: "domestic exile." We may be surprised at the left's clamor to claim this designation, especially if free health care is included in the deal.

Much has been said of the millions of Americans who after September 11 made a point of displaying the stars and stripes from their homes, apartment balconies, and auto bumpers. Less was said—precious little—about leftist intellectuals who refused to fly the flag (and often made a point of reviling those who did) because they saw the flag as a betrayal of their cosmopolitan, sophisticated "I am in America but not of America" individualism. Post–September 11 the firmly entrenched left intelligentsia was unwilling to imagine a form of American patriotism other than the follow-the-leader variety that they had learned to loathe.

This failure of imagination was not new; it had merely lain dormant during the prosperity of the Reagan and Clinton years (during which time many of the trust-fund liberals came into the resources that give them not only this categorical identity but the marvelous freedom to enjoy the type of luxury to which they are opposed with such charming hypocrisy).

With characteristic ingenuity, the radical left of the 1960s, while formally rejecting patriotism based on membership in the

American nation, succeeded in turning their refusal to join up into a new counterculture communalism based on the virtues of not becoming a member of the predominant culture. This new, nonmembership membership entailed fundamental opposition to authority, power, and hierarchy of any kind. (It is entirely possible that one of the main reasons the 1960s' so-called youth movement fell apart was the sheer number of hours activists spent in planning meetings ensuring that everyone got the same amount of time to speak about the badness of the System.) This sixties pack mentality in the name of precious, morally superior individualism soon developed into a gleefully paradoxical tradition of antitraditionalism. The war in Vietnam became the movement's focal point, and moral equivalence became the name of the game.

No idea is more basic to the left than the tenet that truth is spoken only at the edges, by the alienated, the disenfranchised, the marginalized, the beaten down. The left's sixties-era battle cry "Never trust anyone over thirty" found Woodstock-inspired undergraduates declaring that they would study only those subjects they found "personally relevant." This inevitably morphed into a pervasive and insidious contempt for all ideas, literature, and religions handed down by ancestors and elders. Amazingly, accomplished leftists today approaching social security eligibility insist that they remain outsiders to the power structure. Many do so as leading journalists, academicians, and political brokers. Ironically, these posers now personify the very authority figures they detested when the authority was wielded by evil university presidents, military officers, and other older-than-thirty movers and shakers who were always little more than symbolic stand-ins for their unresolved anger toward Dad—you know, that beleaguered guy who busted his rear end making money so his ecologically superior children could go study Zen, practice windsurfing, and attend human potential workshops on the evils of capitalism.

The radical left's hatred of the nation that gives them refuge is ultimately an expression of a self-loathing whose depth is hard to fathom, especially considering the large number of MoveOn.org check writers whose discretionary wealth is made possible by trust funds established by parents and grandparents for whom the free-enterprise system represented not oppression but opportunity. Festering resentment, ingrown anger, and inconsolable guilt seem to be the left's standard psychological response to the economic and political promise that America alone represents in the world. "Feelings of guilt tend to turn into feelings of hatred and contempt," noted the English lawyer and writer Owen Barfield. "We may feel a bit guilty ourselves, but we are very sure that a whole lot of other people are much more guilty, and probably ought to be destroyed." Hence the scarcely contained glee of so many on the left who rushed to blame America for the September 11 attacks, along with Senator John Kerry's contemptible declaration that he is "glad" if CIA operative Mary McCarthy surreptitiously violated her oath, broke the law, leaked classified secrets and lied about it.

By the mid-1970s the left's outsider posture had become permanent body language. This was apparent in the curiously casual tone of their post–September 11 proposals: Find out what "really" motivated the suicide pilots; invite the United Nations to collect evidence against bin Laden; organize international trials; and so on. The greatest danger after September 11 was not that we would get struck again, but that "the authorities" would use the tragedy to implement their long-planned suspension of civil liberties, rounding up the usual suspects at long last—or perhaps more accurately, rounding up the suspects yet again. It is standard practice on the American left to interpret national self-defense as a prelude to domestic repression. To be sure, spirited defense of civil liberties has an important place at times of national emergency. Yet the left's rush to take up the civil liberties banner made all the more plain their nonchalance toward the idea that the country also faced real dangers. How much more compelling the left's critique, say, of Bush's response, would have sounded if proposals from the left made it clear that self-defense and civil liberties are not mutually exclusive.

But that kind of response—intrinsically responsible and geared to protect America in the fullest sense—was not the far left's true concern. The goal was to oppose the authorities, yet again. "Not in my name" became the watchword of the newly reconstituted "peace" movement. Translation: Whatever America is doing, we're not part of it. We stand over here, and though we may be a minority, we're righteous and bold and unwavering, if we do say so ourselves.

Flag? You want me to fly the flag? The flag that once defended slavery, and genocide against the American Indians, and imperialism throughout the world? Not a chance I'll fly that flag.

I hasten to add that not every American who opposed our involvement in Vietnam flew foreign flags or burned America's, or rooted for the victory of our nation's enemies. Many of us simply believed the war was wrong, and we pledged to do what we could to bring it to an end. Neither am I dismissing the positive developments that characterize the sixties. At its best, the boomer generation ushered in values that had never been explored on a large-scale basis: pluralism, equality, diversity, noninstitutional spirituality, multiculturalism—hence, a greater concern for marginalized perspectives and groups, civil rights, feminism, ecology, cross-cultural studies.

But there was a hidden toxic undercurrent to this otherwise healthy shift: a runaway relativism that went beyond respecting previously marginalized groups, to declaring that all forms of hierarchy, all conventional norms, all established structures of authority—especially Mom and Dad—are necessarily and intrinsically oppressive. We can all giggle at newsreels of this antiauthority, antihierarchy, antimodernity worldview at Woodstock, but the continuing problem is that this form of consciousness became a virulent ideology that today goes by the pretentious name of deconstructive postmodernism.

Today's moral equivalence movement can be traced to these developments. The catechism goes like this: "Cultures different from America's must be judged on their own terms because there is no basis for making distinctions between cultures, because distinctions are judgmental and hierarchical and based on hidden power advantages enjoyed by mainstream, dominator cultures." This is absurd on its face, simply because the assertion that there's no basis for universal value judgments is itself a universal value judgment pretending not to be.

America has not always lived up to its creed. To the contrary, when this nation has fallen short, as with slavery and segregation and second-class status for women, the fall has been egregious. What most validates the American democratic quest is its genius for self-correction. When we get things wrong, we work to set things right. More than any other quality, this is what makes the phrase "American exceptionalism" not an abstract theory but a self-evident fact, confirmed in the best scientific sense by countless experimental trials.

It goes without saying that love of country is real for a great many Americans who play politics left of center. Faith in government activism is not somehow intrinsically at odds with patriotism. Many of the most outraged voices in the wake of September 11 were those of liberals in the classical sense of the word. Salman Rushdie wrote movingly about the need to "be clear about why this bien-pensant anti-American onslaught is such appalling rubbish. Terrorism is the murder of the innocent; this time, it was mass murder. To excuse such an atrocity by blaming U.S. government policies is to deny the basic idea of all morality: that individuals are responsible for their actions." Left-wing dissident Christopher Hitchens assailed his comrades as "soft on crime and soft on fascism," later declaring that he wanted no alliance with leftists who believed John Ashcroft to be a greater threat to American freedom than Osama bin Laden.

In the same spirit, the NAACP issued an equally forceful "message of resolve," declaring, "These tragedies and these acts of evil must not go unpunished. Justice must be served." Kim Gandy, president of the National Organization for Women, gave no indication that she or her group were mired in Barbara Ehrenreich's ambivalence. Gandy stated, "The Taliban government of Afghanistan, believed to be harboring suspect Osama bin Laden, subjugates women and girls, and deprives them of the most basic human rights—including education, medicine and jobs. The smoldering remains of the World Trade Center are a stark reminder that when such extremism is allowed to flourish anywhere in the world, none of us is safe."

These few bold responses, however, do not change the fact that for over three decades the cultural left's center of gravity has shifted decisively toward the conviction that America is synonymous with an unending series of crimes and depredations against humanity. Two recent examples deserve mention.

When Senator Ted Kennedy pronounced that Abu Ghraib had "reopened under new management," his obvious premise was that there is no way to distinguish the despicable actions of rogue guards from the unspeakably systematic genocide of Saddam Hussein. Meanwhile, documentary filmmaker Michael Moore actually applauded the bombers and beheaders of the Sunni Triangle: "Iraqis who have risen up against the occupation are not 'insurgents' or 'terrorists' or 'the Enemy.' They are the *revolution*, the Minutemen, and their numbers will grow—and they will win."

The name of this game is moral equivalence. Sometimes the best way to learn a game is by actually playing. In that spirit, a few comments are in order about how people and cultures actually develop.

Self-styled progressives ("communist" and "socialist" have such unfortunate connotations) are invariably happy to acknowledge that material and economic resources are often unequally distributed, both within societies and between nations. Individuals and nations do not develop materially at the same rate, and obviously not all cultures are today at the same stage of economic development. There is little reticence on the left when it comes to identifying and articulating economic disparities that foster human suffering (especially if the disparities can be blamed on the United States).

Do not suggest, however, that the distribution of moral and ethical resources might be similarly uneven. Such a suggestion will not be understood as coherent. People act badly not because of interior choices they make but because oppressive external circumstances leave them no alternative. Redistribute wealth and privilege and restructure class; people will do the right thing. It is really all quite simple.

So, for instance, all people who strap dynamite to their backs and turn themselves into suicide bombers do so because they have been driven to desperation by poverty. This raises some interesting questions. Where were the suicide bombers during America's Great Depression? When the dot-com bubble burst at the start of this century, why didn't unemployed telecommunications workers wire their laptops with explosives and use CEOs as human shields?

Try this: American society, as a whole, has developed beyond the blood-red barbarism of the twelfth century. The Islamist cultures of bin Laden and Zarqawi have not. The West passed through a dynamic fulcrum called the Enlightenment. The Islamic world has not undergone a comparable transformation. Owing to that collective psychic experience, Americans are inheritors of a cultural tradition that passed from medievalism through an unprecedented stage of collective psychic development, culminating in a culture where individual freedom and self-determination constitute treasured values. As a result, individual freedom and self-determination are treasured values, and conflicts are resolved by reason and argument rather than by recourse to custom, authority, and prejudice. Where women and men are viewed as social and civic equals. Where tolerance for different lifestyles and cultures is enthusiastically defended. Where "show me" is street talk for the marvels of empirical proof. And where (Senator Kennedy, take note) when prison scandals get exposed, prosecutions follow.

This is not to say America is immune from error. The Enlightenment is not a vaccination from inhumanity or a guarantee of the millennium in the morning. Yet it borders on the fantastic to deny that there are fundamentally different baseline moral and ethical norms in the United States compared with the cultures of bin Laden and Zarqawi, where "so many Muslims are eager to turn themselves into bombs these days because the Koran makes this activity seem like a career opportunity," writes Sam Harris in his recent book *The End of Faith.*

The Enlightenment is a living tradition today because it consists of standards by which we as Americans agree to judge ourselves in the eyes of the world—standards by which America consistently commits to setting things right when our policies fall short of our ideals and deviate from solid principles. It's about self-correction.

In that regard, America's history of slavery continues to haunt our conscience, as it haunts all cultures and societies that participated in this practice. Slavery is an institution that has existed since the dawn of human history. All types of societies, without exception—including tribal foraging, horticultural, and agrarian—had some degree of slavery. Here's what's amazing. During a one-hundred-year period, from 1780 to 1880, slavery was legally abolished by every industrial nation on earth. What is unique about Western culture is abolition. In no culture other than the West have people eligible to be slaveholders banded together to end the institution.

Listen to the words of Zora Neale Hurston, speaking in 1928:

> I am colored . . . But I am not tragically colored. There is no great sorrow dammed up in my soul, nor lurking behind my eyes. I do not mind at all. I do not belong to the sobbing school of Negrohood who hold that nature somehow has given them a lowdown dirty deal and whose feelings are all hurt about it. Even in the helter-skelter skirmish that is my life, I have seen that the world is to the strong regardless of a little pigmentation more or less. No, I do not weep at the world—I am too busy sharpening my oyster knife.
>
> Someone is always at my elbow reminding me that I am the granddaughter of slaves. It fails to register depression with me. Slavery is sixty years in the past. The operation was successful and the patient is doing well, thank you. . . . I am off to a flying start and I must not halt in the stretch to look behind and weep. Slavery is the price I paid for civilization, and the choice was not with me. It is a bully adventure and worth all that I have paid through my ancestors for it. No one on earth ever had a greater chance for glory. The world to be won and nothing to be lost.

Thomas Jefferson declared that all men are created equal, yet he owned slaves. The left says his slaveholding cancels his credibility about human rights, but Jefferson was not the first human being whose visionary skills were better developed than his moral sensibility. His talk was ahead of his walk. His talk was right, and the West has led the way in implementing those words in the real world.

Jefferson didn't apologize, but then neither did Al Sharpton. Both men ran for president, so let's start from there. Sharpton became famous for his 1987 involvement in a hoax perpetrated by a young black teenager named Tawana Brawley, who claimed to have been kidnapped and raped by several white men. During the ensuing media frenzy, Sharpton accused a local prosecutor, Steve Pagones, of taking part in the raping of Brawley. A subsequent investigation determined that she had fabricated the charges. Pagones sued Sharpton over falsely accusing him of participating in the alleged rape. In 1998 Pagones won a $345,000 judgment against Sharpton and two of his advisers. Sharpton has yet to apologize or indicate any remorse for smearing Pagones.

Sharpton went on to be convicted in 1993 for failing to file a New York State tax return. In 1995, Sharpton publicly railed against a Jewish shopkeeper as a "white interloper." Three months later, seven of the store's employees were murdered in what police called racially motivated killings. In 2002 Sharpton was evicted from the Empire State Building for failing to pay his rent. Two years later he entered the Democratic Party's contest for president.

My comparison between Jefferson and Sharpton may appear to be something of a stretch. After all, Jefferson is dead; how can he be expected to apologize? Fair point. Larger point: Since apologies for wrong actions are so valued on the left, and since the left is the bastion of altruism and public-minded goodness, there's still time for Al Sharpton to admit the error of his ways.

After slavery the left invariably turns its sights to American Indians as victims of genocide. But history records that most Indians died not in warfare but of diseases against which they had no immunity, diseases that the American colonists did not know-ingly spread. This is different from genocide. Sadly for the left's agenda, epidemiology and ideology don't always mesh.

This leaves colonialism. The idea that the West invented colo-nialism shows an abysmal ignorance of history. Consider India, where the English were among the most recent colonialists. When Gandhi sent the British packing, what happened? Indians chose to retain and adopt key Western assumptions and practices, such as the legal tradition of "innocent until proven guilty" and other "foreign" concepts like "rights," "liberty," and "sovereignty." Amazing: The formerly colonized "oppressed" people decided they wanted to man-age their own affairs, but hey, thanks for the civilizing influences like "the rule of law."

Left-wing multiculturalists love to romanticize the tolerance of so-called indigenous peoples. However, anthropology shows that most such cultures are highly ethnocentric—focused on "our group" and hostile to other tribes. The very Western culture that the left despises is the first culture in the world with moral norms that make it possible to question the identification of the good with getting one's own way—the first culture to practice plural-ism. That ability to take the view of the other is what makes this nation the most genuinely tolerant place on the planet.

Here's the delicious irony: The leftist academics who romanti-cize ethnocentric primal cultures are able to do so precisely thanks to Western moral norms that make it possible to value "the other." The left then turns around and declares America the most op-pressive nation on earth. For an exercise in hilarity, watch Ameri-can proponents of multiculturalism take on the garb and customs of the exotic cultures that they romanticize. Meanwhile, the young people in those cultures make it clear that they want to move in the direction of the West. And by "the West" I mean the dynamism of a culture that owes its vitality to the confluence of democracy, science, and capitalism. Our standard of living, our intellectual freedom, our cultural innovation are why so many people throughout the world dream of becoming Americans.

The moral relativism left typically responds that there's no valid basis for making universally based value judgments about right and wrong, good and evil. But the deconstructionist credo that universal value judgments lack validity is *itself* a universal value judgment, one that smacks itself upside the head and cancels its own claim. But wait: Is it conceivable that a political and cultural movement calling for the wholesale leveling of privilege and rank would promulgate procedural and philosophical rules for everyone to follow, while exempting itself? Yes, and that's exactly the point. Consistency and intellectual integrity are small beer compared with the euphoria of reflexively blaming America for everything that goes wrong in the world.

Noam Chomsky made famous the phrase "manufacture of consent" to convey his belief that Americans do not freely choose their society's direction; they are the victims of an extensive propaganda machine that ensures that their seeming consent is manufactured. It is an interesting line of reasoning, and no doubt applicable to the practice of Chomsky's followers placing themselves beyond blameworthiness in communities of unanimous thought (Berkeley, Boulder, Austin, Madison, Cambridge, to name a few) devoted to what he would not think to call the "manufacture of dissent." For this is what the American left does—manufactures dissent, protest, alienation, estrangement, oppression—and then the left revels in it. At the end of the day it's hard to beat what Philip Roth, in his novel *I Married a Communist,* described as "the combination of embitterment and not thinking."

When the president of the United States asked Americans to volunteer blood to the Red Cross after September 11, it is worth remembering that he didn't also ask us to volunteer for suicide missions or to enter American mosques and start taking hostages. Here's the money question: Even if asked to do such things, how many of us would say yes? The fact that America's apostles of equivalence can't answer this question without stammering pretty much says it all.

None of this is to say that the radical cultural left doesn't deserve the title "loyal opposition." Their opposition to America is increasingly obvious. To whom or what they are loyal remains less clear.

CHAPTER NINE

DISPLACED DADS

Forcing Fathers to Prove They're Essential

*If a divorced custodial parent "has a good faith reason
to move . . . the custodial parent cannot be prevented,
directly or indirectly, from exercising his or her right
to change the child's residence" unless the noncustodial
parent makes a "substantial showing" that a change of
custody is "essential" to prevent detriment to the children.*

> —California Court of Appeals decision, 2004
> (Ct.App. 1/5 A096012)

If the syntax of the above sentence seems murky, you probably
didn't go to law school. The legal case is about child custody after
divorce, but the case involves much more. It goes to whether we as
a society are prepared to be committed to the idea that the active
involvement of loving fathers is as important to children's well-
being as the active involvement of loving mothers. And if we say
yes to that, are we willing to ensure our beliefs make their way
into how we live, work, play, teach, and pass on worthy values to
future generations?

As a writer I began paying attention to what seemed the absence of fathers long before I became one or ever imagined *father*

could make sense as a verb. In 1990 a publisher invited me to edit an anthology of writings by men on their experience of actually being men. Told I could select all the writings myself, I jumped at the opportunity. On the one hand, the feminist sisterhood had made clear which male qualities were acceptable and which weren't. Phil Donahue and Alan Alda immediately signed on as role models, declaring that males must learn to be gentle, cooperative, nurturing, and communicative. (The primary male task was to learn to accept and embody behaviors traditionally labeled feminine.) At the same time there seemed a near absence of contemporary male perspectives about the stages of male development. It occurred to me that men must somehow have found their way to productive and meaningful adulthood before feminists were around to direct the traffic.

Turns out, my hunch was right. For centuries men have had access to information—call it a domain, in a figurative sense—dealing with mentorship, initiation, rites of passage, spiritual connection with male ancestors. Males unapologetically have the company of other males in recreation, work, education, and yes, in war. It is not quite accurate to say that fathers were traditionally considered indispensable. The absence of fathers was beyond imagination, so no discussion of their "role" took place. What a difference a century or two makes.

My research led me to conclude that the deep longing for fathers in modern culture reflects, in part, the Industrial Revolution's removal of fathers from home life. That era is over, but the marginalization of fathers and fathering continues, aided by dubious (and highly male antagonistic) feminist scholarship, abetted by activist judges who decree that after divorce the primary custodial parent (typically the mom) is entitled to move minor children to a new city, town, or country, unless the noncustodial parent (generally the dad) can show how doing so would not be in the best interests of the children.

Notice the tacit presumption in favor of sidelining dads. It is up to divorced fathers to make the case, as if by a great stretch of reasoning, that in most situations kids might actually do best with both parents actively participating in their lives. Eric Traub is one such dad faced with that big burden of proof.

Two years ago Traub awaited a California Supreme Court ruling that was certain to have a big impact on his legal standing as a father. Traub didn't want his thirteen-year-old daughter, Angelique, to move to Central America with his ex-wife. He believed Angelique would be better off staying at her school in Marin with the kids she knows. And he felt it would be best if she stayed close to him. In the wake of that legal ruling (*Marriage of LaMusga*), Traub is hopeful he and other men in his position are not on their way to becoming displaced dads.

Let's briefly review the key legal facts.

When the California Supreme Court issued a 1996 decision (*Marriage of Burgess*) affirming the right of divorced parents with primary custody to move away with their children, women's rights activists cheered the decree as a historic advance for the rights of mothers. When the same court later issued a ruling (*Marriage of LaMusga*) clarifying *Burgess*, most of the cheers came from fathers' rights advocates and divorced dads, while the feminist California Women's Law Center condemned the decision as "a huge step backwards."

"This decision changes the focus in move-away cases from a parent-centered to a child-centered context," says Traub, founder and teacher of a workshop series called "Eye to I," for eighteen-to-twenty-four-year-olds who are having difficulty making the passage from adolescence to adulthood. "Based solely on *Burgess*, numerous lawyers told me I had practically no chance to remain active in my daughter's life. *LaMusga* gives hope to fathers who know it's wrong to ask a child which parent she wants to give up."

In its landmark April 29, 2004, ruling, the court held that several factors—including the relationship with noncustodial parents—must be considered before children of divorced couples can be moved out of town. The decision refines the eight-year-old *Burgess* ruling that courts had broadly interpreted as giving custodial parents (most of whom are mothers) the "presumptive right" to relocate unless it could be shown to be detrimental to the children's development, including their relationship with the noncustodial parent.

"This area of law is not amenable to inflexible rule," wrote Justice Carlos Moreno, the father of an adopted child. "We must permit our superior court judges . . . to exercise their discretion to fashion orders that best serve the interests of the children in the cases before them."

The underlying clash was between a divorced San Francisco Bay area couple, Susan Navarro and Gary LaMusga. Navarro wanted to move with her new husband and boys—Garrett and Devlen, ages twelve and ten—to Ohio. LaMusga fought the move, arguing it would be harmful to his children because it would destroy their relationship with him. The trial court ruled in the father's favor, ordering a change in custody of the two boys if their mother followed her new husband to Ohio. The First District Court of Appeals reversed, arguing that as long as the move away is not done in "bad faith" (intended to prevent or discourage contact between the kids and the other parent), the custodial parent has every right to move away with her children, unless the father can prove that, in the event of a move, awarding him custody would be essential to his children's well-being.

Declaring "essential" to be an unreasonably high standard, the supreme court ruled that "the likely impact of the proposed move on the non-custodial parent's relationship with the children is a relevant factor in determining whether the move would cause detriment to the children and . . . may be sufficient to justify a change

in custody." The justices voted 6 to 1 to uphold a Contra Costa
County judge's order switching primary physical custody of their
two sons to LaMusga if their mother followed her new husband
to Ohio.

Under *Burgess*, a noncustodial parent had the burden of proving that the planned move of the custodial parent was intended to
frustrate relations between the children and the parent with whom
they spend less time. *LaMusga* is the first high court decision to
turn on the potential harm to children as a result of reduced contact with their father. Other factors that must be considered in
custody change decisions include the children's interest in stability and continuity in the present custodial arrangement; the distance of the move; the age of the kids; the children's relationship
to both parents; the ability of parents to communicate and cooperate effectively and their willingness to put their kids' interests
first; reasons for the proposed move; the extent to which parents
are already sharing custody; and the wishes of the kids (if they're
old enough to weigh in).

Leslie Shear, a Southern California family law specialist in
Encino who filed an amicus brief in behalf of numerous individuals and groups supporting children's rights, says the decision
"fundamentally restores to family law judges the power to consider every factor that bears on the child's well-being in making
individual determinations." She hailed the decision as "an absolute victory for the children."

No way, says Tony Tanke, an attorney who argued for Susan
Navarro. *LaMusga* is "the worst day for children in the history of
California" because "custodial parents—most of whom are mothers, have lost the presumptive right to make decisions to better
their lives and the lives of their children." Tanke calls the decision
"fundamentally lawless" by giving local judges the power to forbid custodial parents from relocating "because they were not sufficiently friendly toward an ex-spouse."

Garrett Dailey, the Oakland lawyer who represented Gary LaMusga, counters, "The Supreme Court probably viewed Susan Navarro's actions more as a matter of bad faith than bad manners. The court's independent evaluator, who followed the case for five years, was unable to name a single thing the mother had done during that time to facilitate or encourage a relationship between Gary LaMusga and his boys." Dailey cites evidence that when LaMusga volunteered at his kids' school in order to spend more time with his boys, Navarro had instructed teachers to keep track of time so she could deduct it from his court-ordered visitation.

In its *LaMusga* ruling the court referred to a discrepancy between Susan Navarro's words and actions: "Although the mother stated that she wanted to move to Ohio because that 'is where she is originally from and where she has family support,' [court psychologist Dr. Philip Stahl] suggested an additional motive: 'Underneath, however, it has always appeared that [the mother] has wanted to move so that she can remove herself and the boys from the day-to-day interactions with [the father]. She has difficulty dealing with him and prefers to have as little communication with him as possible.'"

Dailey opened his court case with this question: "What happens when the desires of the custodial parent conflict with the child's best interest?" He says the justices reached the reasonable conclusion that the children would be better served by not moving away from their father, their friends, their school, their environment. The case is neither a father's rights victory nor antimother, Dailey says. "*LaMusga* does nothing to change the fact that custodial parents still have a presumptive right to move, if the move is for good reason and good faith, and if the custodial parent has fostered a good relationship between the other parent and the child." Dailey believes it comes down to the fact that *LaMusga* will provide a more level playing field for all such cases in the future.

Eric Traub and Tina Brenes divorced in 1995, when their daughter was five. Brenes had primary custody of Angelique; Traub had unlimited visitation rights. All three moved together twice—first to Southern California, then to the Bay Area. Brenes remarried three years ago, and decided two months later to move to Costa Rica with her daughter (now fourteen) and new husband, who had left Costa Rica at age four and now wanted to retire to his country of birth. (Brenes and her attorney, Kim Robinson, did not respond to repeated requests to be interviewed for this book.)

"Tina and I have a fundamental disagreement about the likely impact on our daughter of a move to Costa Rica," says Traub, who spends just under half of each week with his daughter, including driving her to and from school and helping her with homework. "Living in another country can be an expanding experience, but not at this time. Especially as a child of divorce, she needs stability and continuity."

Believing litigation wouldn't be in their daughter's best interests, Traub offered to pay for mediation, and invited his former wife to choose a mediator she trusted. Brenes declined the offer and served Traub with legal papers stating her intention to move to Costa Rica with Angelique. Both parents agreed on an independent court evaluator, who did an exhaustive two-year investigation of both family units, serving as their daughter's agent in court. The evaluator concluded that for Angelique to move at this time would be "highly detrimental" to her development.

The presiding judge subsequently called both parties to chambers and recommended they not go to trial—standard procedure, because an official court evaluator's recommendations carry great weight in custody disputes. Brenes opted for a trial, filing a brief arguing that she and her daughter could enjoy a higher standard of living in Costa Rica, live in a safer environment, and have the backing of her new husband's extended family. Brenes conceded in court that a move to Costa Rica wasn't in her daughter's best interests at present. She expressed confidence that Angelique would learn Spanish and adapt well to the new location, and still visit her father in California a couple of times a year.

In 2003, a Contra Costa County trial court affirmed the evaluator's opinion: Not now. Brenes could move with Angelique in two years at the soonest, if Angelique wanted to make the move. The court emphasized the importance of Angelique's finishing with the school she's in. Brenes filed an immediate appeal questioning the court's competence to decide the matter, saying she had no intention to move without Angelique.

Traub is one of the more engaged, hands-on dads you'll ever meet. "Since my divorce nine years ago, I have moved three times, following Tina around California, in order to be close to my daughter and so she could have both parents nearby. I supported Tina financially so she would not have to work for six years after we split, and still maintained a balanced visitation schedule of having my daughter with me at least forty percent of the time. Angelique has always understood the implications of the move, which is why she has always been against it. She has no reluctance to discuss it with me, because I am the one who has been fighting for her voice to be heard."

Traub says he definitely wants his daughter to see the world, when the time is right to do so. "However, more importantly I want Angelique to have both loving parents in her life. Even though from a legal standpoint I opposed the move, in spirit I have never fought *against* anything in this matter. I have always been and will always be fighting for my daughter's voice to be heard, for her healthy development, for her strength and fulfillment as a woman." Even if he had been willing to move to Costa Rica with Brenes and her husband, Traub notes that the court psychologist in the case concluded that such a move would be detrimental to their daughter at this time. "Angelique also feels this and only wants her needs and desires to be heard," Traub

says. "I think that listening to our children is the highest imperative of all, and that's what all of this really boils down to."

Contrary to widespread media reports that the supreme court
had reversed *Burgess,* the court said *LaMusga* was intended to
reaffirm and spell out its prior *Burgess* ruling. Both decisions emphasized that the paramount consideration in move-away custody
cases must be the child's best interest—a phrase that appears repeatedly in both rulings.

When parents can't agree, courts invariably look to the informed opinion of expert witnesses. Many observers believe the
decisive factor in Gary LaMusga getting custody of his two sons
(if his ex-wife moves to Ohio) was a seminal shift of opinion
among social science researchers about what's best for kids in relocation cases—a shift that crystallized in the eight years between
the two Supreme Court decisions.

In *Burgess,* the court gave considerable weight to a brief submitted by Marin psychologist and researcher Judith Wallerstein,
author of *The Unexpected Legacy of Divorce,* an anecdotal account
of the long-term effects of divorce on some one hundred children.
Wallerstein's brief emphasized the fundamental importance of
maintaining the stability and continuity of "a family unit" com-
prising the primary custodial parent and his or her children—now
known as the "primary psychological parent" doctrine. Wallerstein argued that the custodial parent is the central influence on
children's adjustment and that "frequent and continuing contact
between the father and child is not a significant factor in the child's
psychological development."

Wallerstein is legendary for the "ditch dad" spirit she brings to
her work as a writer and activist for women's rights issues. When
she reprised the same basic argument in the *LaMusga* case, a coun-
terbrief was filed by Richard Warshak, a clinical professor of

psychology at the University of Texas Southwestern Medical Center. Insisting that Wallerstein's brief had ignored a large body of evidence discrediting the notion that children have only one psychological parent, Warshak (along with twenty-eight divorce researchers, authors, and psychologists) argued that it's crucial for courts to take into consideration the nonresidential parent and child as another family unit that also warrants stability and continuity.

Dr. Joan Kelly of Corte Madera, a coauthor of the Warshak brief, has focused since 1970 on research in children's adjustment to divorce, custody and access issues, divorce mediation, and applications of child development research to custody and access decision making. Kelly believes one of the main problems with the primary psychological parent doctrine is its basis in theory rather than empirical research.

"We know now that children develop attachments at a very young age to both parents, beginning as early as seven months," says Kelly, author of *Surviving the Breakup: How Children and Parents Cope with Divorce.*

There's a fairly new body of sound research that shows both parents are important to the child. The relationships may have different meanings, and each relationship is unique. The primary psychological parent theory ignores the fact that children have different parental needs depending on their ages and stage of development. The situation is fluid. Another shortcoming of the primary psychological parent theory is its general failure to distinguish between parental conflict related specifically to a planned move-away and conflict between the parents as individuals.

Kelly is concerned about the drop-out rate in fathering caused in part by institutional barriers that prevent divorced fathers from having sufficient time to spend with their children. "Two weekends per month with kids is not enough. These schedules make the relationship less meaningful to both father and child." Moving after divorce may interfere substantially with the contacts and relationships between children and their nonmoving parents, Kelly says.

> When we talk about moving away with young children, depending on issues such as distance, we're very often talking about the end of the relationship between the child and the noncustodial parent. Research on the impact of actively involved fathers postdivorce shows that when fathers continue to provide appropriate discipline to the child, get involved in school projects, offer guidance and nurturing to kids, the kids thrive. In such situations, we don't see any difference between the children of divorce and the children of married couples. So what's important is a meaningful contribution to the child's life by both parents after separation.

This obviously doesn't apply to fathers and mothers who are uninterested, abusive, or otherwise toxic in their influence, Kelly adds.

Critics of the *LaMusga* ruling vow to fight on for the rights of custodial parents to move in order to create a better life elsewhere for themselves and their kids. In effect, mothers are trapped, says Kim Robinson, the lawyer who represents Brenes's appeal. "Fathers and husbands own their children and own their wives and ex-wives and control their destinies," Robinson told a reporter for the *San Jose Mercury News*. "A father who hasn't paid attention to the kids for years can say his ex-wife can't move, because if she does move it will mean he won't be able to have a relationship with the kids. It's crazy."

Traub laughs at the idea that he "owns" his ex-wife and daughter. He says "the beauty of the *LaMusga* ruling is that it states unequivocally that the best interests of the child have equal weight with the desires of the parents." He gets quiet for a moment, then continues. "At the height of the legal wrangling, here's what I said to Angelique. If you want to be here, I promise to win this battle for you. And if I lose—if I can't keep my promise—I will pack up tent, give up my career here in the States, and I will move to Costa Rica so you can have both Mom and Dad with you."

The larger issue in these disputes is whether we are prepared as a culture to recognize and support the importance of children of divorce retaining the loving bonds they share with both parents. In a recent ruling (*Brown v. Yana*) the California Supreme Court ruled that Anthony Yana, who was trying to prevent his then twelve-year-old son from being moved from central California to Las Vegas, did not merit an evidentiary hearing on how the move will affect his son. The decision creates another obstacle for non-custodial parents who want to prevent their children from being moved out of their lives.

Consider how the debate would be framed if men, not women, were the primary custodial parent in most postdivorce families, and if those fathers regularly proposed to move their young children vast distances that would severely diminish the mother's opportunity to play an active role in their kid's life. It's a sure bet we would hear volumes about "society's war against divorced mothers" and "the power of patriarchy to affirm the prerogatives of men over the child-rearing role that mothers have assumed for centuries," and so on.

In fact, feminist ideologues have made a cottage industry out of dismissing fatherhood as an obsolete gender role. In "Deconstructing the Essential Father," published in the influential *American Psychologist* in 1999, the authors maintained that children are just fine as long as they have "parenting figures" of either sex, who need not be biologically related. Not surprisingly, the authors called for policies supporting the legitimacy of "diverse family structures" rather than "privileging the two-parent, heterosexual, married family."

Urie Bronfenbrenner, a leading scholar in developmental psychology and child rearing, mopped the floor with the dispensable dad thesis. "Controlling for factors such as low income, children growing up in father-absent households are at a greater risk for experiencing a variety of behavioral and educational problems, including extremes of hyperactivity and withdrawal; lack of attentiveness in the classroom; difficulty in deferring gratification; impaired academic achievement; school misbehavior; absenteeism; dropping out; involvement in socially alienated peer groups; and the so-called 'teenage syndrome' of behaviors that tend to hang together—smoking, drinking, early and frequent sexual experience, and in the most extreme cases, drugs, suicide, violence, and criminal acts," Bronfenbrenner wrote in an article entitled "Discovering What Families Can Do."

The issue of displaced fathers in divorce is not chiefly about fathers' rights but about what is best for children and right for society at large. After decades in which the primary place of fathers was the workplace, and home life considered Mom's domain, men are heeding the call to active fathering in unprecedented ways. Kids need dads who are willing to bring the energy, the faith, and the devotion that children need. Radical feminists have worked for decades to strip positive images of fathering from the culture at large. Pandering to this movement, the mainstream media presents continuous imagery of the *immature* or *shadow* father, who is abusive, delinquent, adolescent, unfaithful, addicted.

Rarely do we hear stories about the sacrifices of fathers, the teaching of fathers, the affection of fathers, or the devotion of fathers like Eric Traub and Gary LaMusga. These men aren't heroes. They are adult men dedicated to giving their kids stability, presence, attention, advice, values, and mentoring. They're *dads*. Dispensable? Only if we're prepared to undertake untested social engineering of the kind favored by Professor Katharine Bartlett, a radical feminist scholar and dean of Duke University's law school, who explains that her passion is

> the value I place on family diversity and on the freedom of individuals to choose from a variety of family forms. This same value leads me to be generally opposed to efforts to standardize families into a certain type of nuclear family because a majority may believe this is the best kind of family or because it is the most deeply rooted ideologically in our traditions.

If the syntax of the above passage seems murky, you probably didn't take enough women's studies classes. Bartlett says we dare not "standardize" families in accordance with the two-parent framework that has passed the test of centuries of lived experience and accumulated species wisdom. Columnist Katha Pollitt gets to the point: "Why not have a child of one's own? Children are a joy; many men are not." That probably works for feminist activist Marlo Thomas, whose book and album *Free to Be . . . a Family* teach kids that "if the people whom you live with are happy to see your face, that's a family." So don't worry, be happy; the sisterhood collective is en route.

It's clear that contempt for the very idea of life-affirming masculinity is second nature to leftists who rejoice in the general process that has been going on since Rousseau's infamous call for incessant class warfare. Well, it's one thing—a generally good thing, I believe—to call into question cultural assumptions that put Father on top economically, socially, politically, sexually, personally, and legally. It is quite another thing—intrinsically wrong and terribly destructive—to set in place a social regime that denies the father all authority, stripping him of his presence in the ecology of family life and child rearing.

"The father has lost his prestige, and Eve has dealt herself a new hand," observes Elizabeth Badinter. No surprise that this is cause for rejoicing among animus-driven feminists, at war not only with fathers but with their very nature as women. But so-called progressives less driven by ideology and unmitigated rage would do well to pause before signing on to the growing antifather frenzy. Because the same leveling forces now aiming to remove fathers from the life of our culture are also moving toward mothers, and show no signs of retreating. Thanks in no small part to decades of motherhood-mocking feminism, today "mothers are discounted everywhere," notes Robert Bly. "When mothers and fathers are both dismembered, we will have a society of orphans, or more exactly, a culture of adolescent orphans."

All the better to speed the pace toward a society based on parenting by the state? Sound like a good idea to unleash an American equivalent of China's tidal wave of youth called the Red Guard, which created a Cultural Revolution that dogmatically stripped down its society on a scale unrivaled by any social upheaval our nation has witnessed? Yes to both questions only if we're prepared to admit we're serious about committing social suicide. At the very least, as Kathleen Parker says,

> A society in which women are alone, men are lonely, and children don't have fathers is nothing to celebrate. And a future world filled with fatherless children—bereft of half their identity and robbed of a father's love, discipline and authority—won't likely be a pleasant place to live.

No kidding.

CHAPTER TEN

KILLING FOR CONVENIENCE

Terri Schiavo's Natural Right to Life

The Terri Schiavo case landed at a federal appeals court Tuesday after a lower court rejected her parents' plea to keep their brain-damaged daughter alive. . . . Schindler spokesman Gary McCullough called the decision "extremely cruel." . . . "Here's a woman whose life is hanging. She's being slowly starved. . . ."

—CNN, March 23, 2005

Before I had ever heard of Terri Schindler Schiavo, I largely agreed with friends and neighbors who believe that each of us has the right to die with dignity, along with the right to stipulate that heroic medical interventions shall not extend life by artificial means. By the day Terri died, I had crossed the street to stand with other friends and neighbors who strongly oppose self-determined dying in assisted suicide and euthanasia. The street is metaphoric, but the distance between the two sides is real and seemingly vast. There are good and decent people lining both flanks, and more than a few others in the center boulevard trying to find their own ground in one of the most difficult debates our nation faces.

The drama that unfolded at the Florida hospice decisively

influenced my thinking about assisted suicide. The only person more amazed than my friends was myself—not being remotely accustomed to agreeing with the likes of Randall Terry, the controversial antiabortion activist who became one of Terri's most passionate defenders. The wedge issue—the distinction that opened a new pathway between my head and heart—was *consent*. There was simply too much conflicting evidence, including Michael Schiavo's contradictory statements, to believe with confidence that depriving Terri of the nutrients crucial to survival was what she would have wanted if she had known she would become unable to care for herself. Terri's parents and siblings were so clearly willing to buy out Terri's death sentence with their commitment to assume full care of her for the rest of her life. Why was this not allowed to happen?

Asked why he persisted in his decade-long effort to end his wife's life despite the wishes of Terri Schiavo's parents and others who love her, Schiavo said: "Because this is what Terri wanted. This is her wish." This statement was at odds with one he had made under oath four years earlier. During a deposition of September 27, 1999, attorney Pamela Campbell—who represented Terri's parents—asked Schiavo, "Have you considered turning the guardianship over to [Robert and Mary] Schindler?" and he answered, "No, I have not." Asked why he wouldn't, Schiavo answered, "Basically, I don't want to do it."

When Campbell pressed him to be more specific, Schiavo declared, "Because they put me through pretty much hell the last few years. . . . Just their attitude towards me because of the litigations. There is no other reason. I'm Terri's husband and I will remain guardian." Asked by Larry King if he understood her family's feelings, Schiavo said: "Yes, I do. But this is not about them, it's about Terri. And I've also said that in court. We didn't know what Terri wanted, but this is what we want."

I believe it was wrong to put Terri Schiavo to death barring clear and convincing evidence that this is what she wanted. Yes, Florida courts had ruled that she was debilitated and beyond repair. A majority of doctors had concluded that she was in a "persistent vegetative state." Under Florida statutes Terri Schiavo had no legal right to live. But the constitution of her state says, "All natural persons, female and male alike, are equal before the law and have inalienable rights, among which are the right to enjoy and defend life and liberty."

The extreme disability of Terri Schiavo did not make her less of a "natural person" than before the tragic developments that left her in a severe state of diminished capacity. Americans who believe in the rule of law accepted the legal verdict with dismay, but many remained convinced that Terri Schiavo had a *natural right to life*. That is my own view. I believe Terri was wrongly deprived of that right by a government that failed to keep its most solemn promise, namely to "secure . . . certain unalienable rights, that among these are life, liberty and the pursuit of happiness."

Death with dignity. At first glance—like on a bumper sticker—the phrase is hard to argue with. Especially considering alternatives like "It's wrong to extend life in grotesque and artificial ways using advanced technology that the terminally ill person would not want," which would require a wide bumper and awfully small print. "The right to die" is another phrase that made sense at first hearing, and second, and third. One day, as an undergraduate, I joined a lively conversation to argue that laws that forbid suicide are absurd. "What, if the suicide's unsuccessful the person will be fined? How many botched attempts before an arrest?" Letting people make their own choices appealed to my libertarian instincts, my sense that self-determining people should be allowed to make their own choices.

My thinking shifted when a friend (whom I'll call Susan) enacted the punch line of my college scenario by making repeated attempts to end her life—once by throwing herself off a cliff.

Susan survived, though her body was wrecked. Here's the question that bothered me, and still does. If it was her choice and hers alone, why did so many of her pro-choice friends and family work so hard to keep my friend from killing herself, especially given that her repeated attempts at self-annihilation were carefully premeditated? That we loved her and wanted her to stay wasn't the full answer; there was some other factor I couldn't quite articulate, and it disturbed me.

Susan had clearly decided to die. As her health deteriorated, family and friends knew her physical pain was often excruciating. So what kept us from setting aside our desire that she remain part of our world, and one by one communicating, "Yes, we'll miss you but it's okay with us if you want to do this." Apart from not wanting to commit a felony (no small consideration), what prevented any of us from giving her a lethal overdose of drugs? That's how my friend eventually succeeded in ending her days on this earth.

My best sense of why we didn't assist Susan in ending her life is that we knew doing so would be deeply wrong. I believe we understood that life is a gift from evolutionary biology and the procreative child rearing of parents, a gift whose ultimate origins bespeak a profound mystery that far transcends the libertarian "property rights" argument of body ownership that made sense when my pro-choice sympathies were reflexive rather than thought through.

Of course I can only speak for myself. But I like to think my friend—even with what proved to be her enormous will to die—I like to imagine Susan would have found my offer of assistance repugnant and degrading.

Personal feelings can justifiably inform one's intellectual views on euthanasia, but policy considerations must be paramount if other states are to be persuaded (as I hope they will be) that Oregon's Death with Dignity Act is the wrong way to care for individuals facing terminal illness or severe disability. The act permits physicians to write prescriptions for a lethal dosage of medication to people with a terminal illness. The law states that in order to participate a patient must be eighteen years of age or older; a resident of Oregon; capable of making and communicating health care decisions for him/herself; and diagnosed with a terminal illness that will lead to death within six months. It is up to the attending physician to determine whether these criteria have been met.

The Oregon law "is the latest result of our failure to develop a better response to the needs of the terminally ill," says Herbert Hendin, executive director of the American Suicide Foundation in New York City. "Fear of dying in unbearable pain or of being kept alive in intolerable circumstances leads a frustrated public to action that only compounds the problem. . . . It is impossible to predict with certainty that a patient has only six months to live, which makes mistaken or falsified predictions inevitable." The big danger is that this "permits assisted suicide when patients are neither in physical pain nor imminently about to die, and will encourage people who fear death to take a quicker way out," Hendin says.

Oregon was not the beginning of state-sanctioned suicide in the name of mercy. The euthanasia track record of the Netherlands should give pause to all who believe the value of life is intrinsic rather than merely instrumental to social and ideological considerations.

In fall 2000 the Dutch parliament voted to formally legalize the practice of euthanasia, making the Netherlands the first nation in the world to do so. (For decades, assisted suicide was practiced in the Netherlands on an informal basis under an ambiguous agreement between the government and the medical association.) Dutch physician Richard Fenigsen has written that Dutch general practitioners perform an estimated five thousand to twenty thousand cases per year, which he notes that in American terms would be from eighty thousand to three hundred thousand cases per year.

The law specifies the conditions under which euthanasia can take place.

The patient must have an incurable illness, but the patient need not actually be dying to be euthanized.

· The patient must be experiencing "unbearable suffering."
· The patient is of sound mind and has given consent.
· Doctors will administer "medically appropriate"
means to terminate life.

Despite the fears of many who believe Dutch society and medicine are on a "slippery slope," euthanasia proponents in the Netherlands say there's little need for concern. Health Minister Els Borst argues that Dutch euthanasia has appropriate safeguards against abuse, insisting that euthanasia will remain a last resort for those who otherwise would face suffering. Somewhat surprisingly, Fenigsen says the Dutch are not on a slippery slope, but he gives a different reason: "Dutch doctors who practice euthanasia are not on a slope. From the very beginning they have been at the bottom."

Fenigsen says his research shows "involuntary euthanasia . . . is rampant." He found that "a staggering 62 percent of all newborns' and infants' deaths resulted from 'medical decisions,'" and that in 1995 alone there were 900 lethal injections given to patients who had not requested euthanasia. Among that group, 189 were fully competent and could have been consulted about their consent, but were not. "Those who contend that it is possible to accept and practice 'voluntary' euthanasia and not allow involuntary totally disregard the Dutch reality," he says.

Fenigsen's grim assessment of euthanasia in Holland even before legalization is supported by the research of an American
team led by Herbert Hendin, published in the *Journal of the
American Medical Association*. Hendin and his associates found:

> From our point of view there has been an erosion of
> medical standards in the care of terminally ill patients
> in the Netherlands. The 1990 and the 1995 studies doc-
> ument that 59 percent of Dutch physicians do not re-
> port their cases of assisted suicide and euthanasia, more
> than 50 percent feel free to suggest euthanasia to their
> patients, and about 25 percent admit to ending patients'
> lives without their consent. How is it that the Dutch
> researchers are so sanguine about their data?

Fenigsen is alarmed by Dutch public opinion surveys that
strongly support society's right to cut short a person's life. "There
is considerable public acceptance of the view that life-saving treatment should be denied to the severely handicapped, the elderly,
and perhaps to persons without families," says Fenigsen. "Further, opinion polls show that a majority of the same public that
proclaims support for voluntary euthanasia, freedom of choice,
and the right to die also accepts involuntary active euthanasia—
that is, denial of free choice and of the right to live."

Why Holland? Fenigsen notes that Dutch medical, legal, and
theological thought was influenced by German thinkers

> who introduced the concept of lives unworthy of being
> lived, and advocated the extermination of useless indi-
> viduals to relieve society of that burden. Appearing on
> the scene half a century after their German predeces-
> sors, after the experience of Nazi euthanasia on psy-
> chiatric patients and the handicapped, after Europe's

historical experience of genocide, and at a much further advanced stage in the development of the Western concept of human rights, the champions of euthanasia in the Netherlands had to present a modified and highly refined program.

Emphasizing the right to die as a human rights issue in the best interest of those who were ill and unhappy influenced growing Dutch support for euthanasia, Fenigsen says. "The other theme, that of the right to kill in the interest of the society, has been downplayed but never actually eliminated, so as not to discourage those who believe that the human race should be improved by the extermination of weaklings. Thus, the prerequisite for the success of the pro-euthanasia movement in Holland has been its extremely well-constructed program."

" 'Voluntary' euthanasia should be rejected because [it] is often counterfeit and always questionable," Fenigsen continues.

Doctors have tried to coerce patients, and wives have coerced husbands, and husbands wives to undergo "voluntary" euthanasia. But it is not these flagrant incidents that matter, it is all the others. For twenty years the population of Holland has been subjected to all-intrusive propaganda in favor of death. The highest terms of praise have been applied to the request to die: This act is "brave," "wise," and "progressive." All efforts are made to convince people that this is what they ought to do, what society expects of them, what is best for themselves and their families. The result is, as Attorney General T.M. Schalken stated in 1984, that "elderly people begin to consider themselves a burden to the society, and feel under an obligation to start conversations on euthanasia, or even to request it."

Fenigsen concludes: "When evaluating the thousands of 'voluntary' requests for euthanasia submitted every year in Holland, one should take into account the influence of propaganda and of the physician provocateur."

Pro-life feminist Sydney Callahan believes women should be especially concerned about the growing acceptance of euthanasia because "women live longer than men, and in their old age command fewer financial and social resources." In a 1995 article in *Studies in Prolife Feminism* she takes issue with the widespread assertion that individuals have a moral right to a self-chosen death by suicide or euthanasia. "Feminists have understood that individuals cannot be treated or treat others as though persons are alienated nomads cut off from all bonds with one another," says Callahan.

Having received the gift of life and social identity, one has moral obligations to preserve and respect each human life and refrain from suppressing, killing or destroying self or others. What is permitted to the self and what is permitted for others to do to a human being cannot be morally or psychologically separated. Murder and suicide are irretrievably linked acts. In ancient cultures such as Rome, where suicide was honored, it was also accepted that powerful elites could unilaterally kill slaves, children or troublesome women. To be a valid protective principle, the moral prohibition against killing a human being must have no exceptions—neither for the self, nor for physicians.

Moreover, the difficulty of determining a person's consent to suicide or euthanasia cannot be overestimated, Callahan says.

Self-knowledge is difficult because the ongoing stream of consciousness is so complex and made up of so many different dimensions. . . . Individual choices, preferences, plans and decisions are never simple or unitary, but exist as ongoing processes. Consciousness is constantly being self-created and re-created; and these individual inner processes are constantly affected by ongoing interpersonal and environmental interactions. . . . Therefore when a conscious decision, or choice, or plan is made to kill one's self, not only must one violently subdue one's body-self, but one must also extinguish all the other implicit stored dimensions of complex personal identity. Other dimensions of personal consciousness may resist dying, and, like the resisting body-self, call for help in the midst of a suicide attempt.

Callahan reports that when people survive suicide attempts or their requests for euthanasia are denied, they often state that they have changed their minds. "They no longer identify with the dimension of self that wanted to die." She adds, "An irreversible conscious decision to end consciousness forever suppresses a core capacity and essential potential of a human being. . . . Death may forcibly take my life away from me, but why give death an easy victory by an irreversible act of self-extinction?"

Philosopher Peter Singer finds these kinds of questions tedious because they privilege human beings in a way that humans don't merit. Princeton University's prestigious Ira W. DeCamp Professor of Bioethics, Singer has been called "the godfather of animal rights," publishing at age twenty-nine *Animal Liberation,* the book that he himself proudly calls "the seminal work of the movement." He famously asked in another book, *In Defense of Animals,* why do we experiment with chimps, "yet would never think of doing the same thing to a retarded human being at a much lower mental level? The only possible answer is that the chimpanzee, no matter how bright, is not human, while the retarded human, no matter how dull, is?"

He explicitly rejects the basic Judeo-Christian tenet that human life is extraordinary, that humans are not comparable to chimps or pigs or rats. "If we compare a severely defective human infant with a nonhuman animal, a dog or a pig, for example, we will often find the nonhuman to have superior capacities, both actual and potential, for rationality, self-consciousness, communication, and anything else that can plausibly be considered morally significant."

Singer has asserted that healthy infants are sentient beings who are neither rational nor self-conscious, and therefore do not count as persons and may be killed. He has no qualms about that word, *killing*, although he thinks too much of it happens to animals, often with cruelty that should shock the conscience of a civilized society. One measure of his test of civilization, it seems, is a capacity to get beyond sappy sentimentality about one's own species. A reporter for *Vegan Voice* magazine asked Singer how he felt about the fact that Singer's "rational argument" for euthanasia hasn't ignited the "revolutionary change you had hoped for." Singer agreed, adding that we humans "are self-interested beings to some extent." Singer told the national Animal Rights 2002 conference in McLean, Virginia, that society should allow a "severely disabled" infant to be killed up to twenty-eight days after its birth if the parents decide the neonate's life is not worth living. Peter Singer "would allow parents and doctors to kill newborns with drastic disabilities (like the absence of higher brain function, an incompletely formed spine called spina bifida, or even hemophilia) instead of just letting nature take its course and allowing the infants to die," the *New York Times* reported.

Shocking? Yes, but again let's be fair. Singer insists that it is never justified to kill a disabled person who *wants* to live—just infants or others who are unable to speak for themselves. (Brings to mind the sixties-era joke—a vegetarian is a person who can't hear a carrot scream.) So when does a member of the human species acquire the status of a person? In his book *Practical Ethics*,

Singer writes: "I propose to use [the term] 'person,' in the sense of a rational and self-conscious being." And so, a "non-person human" is a being who possesses the biological and genetic traits of our species, but who lacks the capacity for the conscious activities typical of those members when they are alert: thinking, feeling, hoping, experiencing pleasure and pain, etc.

But, wait. We're still on the outskirts of Professor Singer's Brave New World of utilitarian thinking. (Utilitarianism is a school of philosophy that insists we have a moral duty to decrease the level of suffering and increase the level of pleasure experienced by as many people as possible, at all costs. Moral absolutes—against killing, in some cases—shouldn't be allowed to stand in the way of this goal.) "What about parents conceiving and giving birth to a child specifically to kill him, take his organs, and transplant them into their ill older children?" That's what a reporter asked Singer. Here is Singer's response: "They're not doing something really wrong in itself."

Is there anything wrong with a society in which children are bred for spare parts on a massive scale? "No," Singer responded.

Not everybody at Princeton agrees with their famous professor's views about the moral neutrality of breeding babies for spare parts. When he received Princeton University's prestigious Ira W. DeCamp professorial slot in bioethics, outraged Princeton students got together a petition that declared: "We protest his hiring because Dr. Singer denies the intrinsic moral worth of an entire class of human beings—newborn children—and promotes policies that would deprive many infants with disabilities of their basic human right to legal protection against homicide."

Attempting to mollify his critics, Singer announced that he opposes discrimination against *adults* with disabilities—unless they can't talk or nod, in which case they would satisfy his definition of "lacking personhood," which would further qualify the disabled adult for a lethal injection. Well, "qualify" may not be the precise word. I suspect "get" a lethal dose of meds is closer—

unless of course the ACLU were to step in and demand an end to such cruel and unusual practices.

In his book *The Expanding Circle,* Singer even criticized Blessed Mother Teresa of Calcutta on grounds that may surprise those who might believe a philosopher would be keenly interested in the nature of unique individuals. Sorry, that's kind of sappy for Peter Singer, who condemned Mother Teresa for (hold on to your hat) describing her love for others as love for each of a succession of individuals rather than as "love for mankind merely as such." "If we were more rational," he says, "we would use our resources to save as many lives as possible, irrespective of whether we do it by reducing the road toll or by saving specific, identifiable lives."

One such life—specific, identifiable—was that of Singer's mother, who became ill with Alzheimer's disease and thereby ceased to meet his definition of a person. She had become a vulnerable, compromised *human nonperson,* in Singer's charming vernacular. Instead of having her killed or leaving her to die (the old Monty Python "Bring out your dead" routine comes to mind), Singer and his sister instead hired a team of home health-care professionals to attend to their ailing mom, in the process spending tens of thousands of dollars that, according to Singer's philosophy, should have been spent reducing the suffering of the greatest number of other people.

Pressed about the apparent contradiction, Singer responded, "I think this has made me see how the issues of someone with these kinds of problems are really very difficult. . . . Perhaps it is more difficult than I thought before, because it is different when it's your mother." Philosopher Peter J. Colosi believes Singer would do well to consider that

> the difference, when the sufferer is your mother, is that you love her. And it is love that opens our eyes to the true source of the worth of persons: their inner

preciousness, unrepeatability, and uniqueness. It is precisely a glimpse of the unrepeatable uniqueness of another human person that inspires love. Once this glimpse is achieved and love springs forth in the soul— as it does like a surprising gift—that love then has the remarkable power of allowing you to see more clearly and deeply the unique preciousness, as well as the humanity, of the person you love. That vision in turn inspires more love. When that happens, there is no philosophical argument that can make you kill the one you love—or in any other way abandon her.

So inconvenient, those "specific, identifiable lives." Nazi Germany's "T 4 Euthanasie" program put to death people with physical and mental disabilities against their will on a systematic basis. No constitutional rights to protect their lives and their liberty. No statutory rights to protect them from discrimination and ensure their personal autonomy. No disability rights/ independent living movement to secure such rights. No guarantee that such rights were enforced.

Could this happen in America? Not easily, and not without a fight, given our constitutional protections and our active disability rights movement. However, it bears remembering that during the first part of the twentieth century disabled individuals were widely viewed in the Western world as flawed, and were treated as second-class citizens. Americans with disabilities were jailed against their will and sterilized without their permission by the physicians from whom they expected medical care.

During Hitler's regime Germany instituted the New Medicine, a health education program that encouraged healthy diets and exercise and discouraged smoking and drinking. "There was also a dark side," writes Hugh Gallagher in the September 22, 2001, issue of the *Journal of Disability Policy Studies*.

People who did not conform to the Nazi standard of a healthy, able-bodied person and who could not be rehabilitated according to those standards were seen as "useless eaters," who "lived lives not worth living." They were "refractory therapy cases," who stood in the way of the "breakthrough campaign" of the New Medicine. Such people should receive "final medical therapy," as part of what the physicians referred to as "negative population policy."

Such persons were to be eliminated from society, from the Volk, explained one of the participating doctors, "out of respect for human life, as I would remove a purulent appendix from a diseased body."

Could this happen in America? Well, more Americans are living longer, healthier, more productively vigorous lives than at any time in our history. Preventive medicine and holistic health care have gone mainstream—yet not without casting a shadow of their own. I find it hard not to shiver when I remember the seemingly wise, apparently compassionate refrain of those who advocated removing Terri Schiavo's feeding tube because she no longer had an acceptable quality of life.

"In Oregon, where assisted suicide is now legal, hospice workers often condone individuals taking lethal overdoses, instead of receiving the ongoing care and concern they deserve," reports N. Gregory Hamilton, an Oregon physician and patient advocate, who is a leader in the state's hospice movement. "This failure to value the lives of vulnerable patients threatens the very basis of Western medicine—a trusting relationship. Many Oregon patients are now expressing fear that the culture of death growing in their state will undermine the core concepts of good palliative care. Many have become afraid to enroll in hospices until the last possible moment. And some patients have become afraid to receive hospice care at all, because they have sensed a shift in the attitude of hospices. This fear threatens the entire palliative care movement. Hospices allowing assisted suicide as an alternative to good care may prove its own death knell."

"Slippery slope" may be an overused metaphor, but that doesn't mean there aren't any. Consider that in the immediate aftermath of *Roe v. Wade* abortion was widely viewed as a tragic and exceptional choice. Today abortion has become routinized and is widely seen as an acceptable form of birth control. "Habituation makes each new case easier to carry out," observes Sydney Callahan. "To my surprise, I once heard Timothy Quill, a prominent physician advocate of assisted suicide, proclaim from a podium that a physician's fourteenth case of assisting a suicide would not be carried through with the same sensitivity as his first case."

Callahan continues, "No one could look unmoved at the abortion rate or contemplate our homicide statistics without a tremor. Unconditional respect for the gift of life is eroding. . . . Under the banner of increasing technological control and increasing liberty— live free or die—we have opened ourselves up to more and more pressures to die."

On June 8, 2002, Carol Carr shot her sons—forty-two-year-old Michael Randy Scott and forty-one-year-old Andy Byron Scott—at their rooms in a Georgia nursing home. Carr pleaded guilty to both shootings, saying she could no longer bear to see her sons suffer from Huntington's disease, a degenerative and hereditary illness.

Have we as a society fallen short of comprehending the plight of our neighbors who suffer severe disabilities or chronic illness? The Georgia tragedy is but one illustration of why the honest answer is yes. Burdened caregivers so often experience enormous sorrow at their burden. But the answer cannot be to condone the murder of the care recipient.

"I need someone every day to help me bathe and move my

limbs and dispose of my bodily wastes," says Mike Ervin, a journalist with muscular dystrophy. "So do I deserve a bullet in the brain?" No, Mike, you don't. And I'm hoping Peter Singer would agree: What was good enough for his mother should be good enough for you.

AFTERWORD

People have asked me if I'm a conservative now. Well, let me answer it this way: I'm no longer a man of the left, but I'm still a liberal—in the original sense of the word.

Say *what*?

"It makes no sense whatever to describe yourself as a liberal who has left the left," a proud progressive from Seattle e-mailed when my essay appeared in the *San Francisco Chronicle*. "If you've become a conservative, just come out and admit it."

Is leaving the left synonymous with moving right? By strict binary logic, the answer seems to be yes. A light switch that isn't on is a light switch that must be off; there can be no other alternative. But not all choices in the real world are limited to sets of mutually exclusive twos. Contrary to popular belief, politics is not a game where the only way to exit the left is to head squarely in the opposite direction, or vice versa.

There's another option. We are free at any time to leap off the left-right line altogether and begin making political choices liberated from the gravity of the ideological continuum, whose pull turns out to be surprisingly escapable.

But as with any freedom, there is a corresponding responsibility. Before leaping it is crucial to know what you value, important to honor what you understand to be true, wise to stay open to surprises and unexpected opportunities for learning. For myself, I departed the left-right line with new clarity about the brilliance of liberal democracy and the value system it entails, the quest for liberty as intrinsically human, and the dangers of demands for adherence to any point of view through silence, fear, or coercion.

And it was only in the wake of leaving that I realized that I had broken away from the conformist imperatives of my hometown for precisely the same reason.

Liberal is one of the most problematic terms around these days. The word comes from the Latin word *liberalis,* meaning "free, befitting a free person." It also means "independent," which is why I refuse to abandon it just because it has become synonymous in the popular mind with its antithesis: schemes for social engineering that issue from elite organizations with self-important initials (ACLU, NAACP, GLAAD, NOW, NARAL, PFAW) that for a growing number of Americans carry all the moral force of EIEIO.

Classical liberalism emerged in the seventeenth and eighteenth centuries as a political philosophy that embraces individual rights and responsibilities, including the right to own and maintain private property against continuous government encroachment. At the heart of original liberalism endures a commitment to tolerance, reason, and self-determination, and a belief that within each person there exists an unassailable right to be free from compulsion. George Washington, James Madison, Thomas Jefferson, Benjamin Franklin, and Thomas Paine risked their lives to create a system of government that places freedom at the core of its concerns and that employs the force of law to secure that freedom from subjugation and tyranny. They believed in the pursuit of happiness as something very much akin to adventure, and they understood that government decrees to guarantee happiness invariably serve to penalize achievers while keeping the poorest among us reliant on minimal subsistence.

"Liberals see inequality and want to make everyone equally miserable," says Rush Limbaugh. Seeking to eradicate all differences in the name of diversity and to suppress human nature in the name of correct thought, the left seeks to return to a mythic age of lost innocence that never existed, trumpeting the attempted regression as progressive. "An atavistic longing after the life of the noble savage," Friedrich Hayek has written, "is the main source of the collectivist tradition."

Yet ultimately the differences between classical liberalism and the contemporary left go far beyond political theory. The key distinctions are played out in the moments in the news that constitute this book.

For instance, America's self-applauding progressives embrace racial preferences as a means of consolidating demographic minorities into a monolithic, victim-based political movement to achieve collective sameness at the expense of individual freedom. By contrast, classical liberals understand that affirmative action contradicts the American idea that individual human beings are the benchmark of ultimate value, hence the actualization of excellence for individuals must be the highest goal and abiding practice of our society.

The authoritarian left embraces Rousseau's conviction that individuals cannot be trusted as stewards of their own destinies in an ownership society. Authentic liberals understand that the unchecked power of the state to confiscate property undermines the sustainability of civil and political freedoms.

Left-wing feminists view gender differences as socially constructed to advance the privileged status of males over females, while genuine liberals champion civil and legal equality for both sexes and declare this commitment in the name of the classical humanistic tradition that grew out of the Enlightenment.

Lockstep leftists condemned Clarence Thomas for "not thinking like a black man should." True liberals viewed his race as irrelevant to his qualifications to sit on America's highest court.

The radical left declares that "women can't be the equal of men unless they are free to rid themselves of their unborn children at any time for any reason," in the words of Kate O'Beirne. Life-affirming liberals insist that the barbaric practice of partial-birth abortion is an affront to the dignity of human life and civilized culture.

The selectively ethical left excused Bill Clinton's lies under oath because lying about sex doesn't really count. Real liberals understand that respect for the rule of law is diminished when elected officials violate their sacred trust for personal expediency.

The raging postmodern left viewed September 11 as an opportunity to advance its campaign to undermine America's standing in the world. Freedom-loving liberals, recognizing that the totalitarian ideology of al Qaeda stands against the very foundations of Western society, cheered the heroic passengers of United flight 93 rather than positing that the suicide pilots must have had bad childhoods.

Social-engineering progressives seized upon the Columbine shootings as additional evidence of the need for more gun laws and politically correct curricula. Real-world liberals refused over-arching generalizations about society's blame, instead urging parents to pay closer attention to what's going on in the lives of their children.

The instrumentalist mentality of the left views physician-assisted suicide as entirely a matter of personal choice, while bona fide liberals share Hubert Humphrey's view that "[t]he moral test of a government is how it treats those who are at the dawn of life, the children; those who are in the twilight of life, the aged; and those who are in the shadows of life, the sick, the needy, and the handicapped."

The list could continue, highlighting the many and stark ways in which the well-founded liberalism that empowers individuals to better themselves and their families in the pursuit of happiness is inherently at odds with the leftist-progressive "inability to come to terms with who we are; the obstinate, compulsive, destructive belief in the fantasy of transformation, in the desperate hope of an earthly redemption," as David Horowitz expresses it so well.

Where does that leave me? Very close in spirit to blogger Jeff Medcalf, who kept getting called a Republican simply because his views sounded "conservative." I share his sense that

> our political lexicon is too limited, too constrained for adequate description. I am a republican, federalist, libertarian, constitutionalist, conservative, classically liberal, capitalist, free-marketeering, free-trading, secular, spiritual, culturally western, tolerant of honest disagreement, advocate of a strong national defense. Notice the lack of capital letters, by the way, on the politically loaded terms. And which of these takes precedence on any given issue depends on the details of the issue. There's not a term for this, other than "independent." But "independent" is itself too limited and too-frequently misused to be a meaningful label. In America, "independent" just means you aren't a Democrat or a Republican.

So I'm standing by my choice: liberalism of the original, nonleft kind. Among other things, this means that the Madison correspondent I mentioned in my Preface, who accused me of selling out, was quite right. Indeed, I've sold all my shares in a worldview that fosters tribal identity and group privilege and bitter communal division in the name of diversity. I've liquidated my stock in a philosophy that empowers a guardian state to encourage learned helplessness and endless class warfare, in the name of equality. I have divested all holdings in the pathological school of pluralism that scorns individual initiative, free enterprise, logic, the Enlightenment, science, Judeo-Christian values, the possibility of objective knowledge, and the necessity of personal responsibility.

The classic liberalism that makes me hopeful for my country's future is one that celebrates the creative power of intrinsic inner intent as the prime factor in individual excellence and cultural innovation. In the final analysis, genuine freedom is not caprice but room to enlarge, to change course midway, to set out on unexpected roads that emerge just past the next bend. This is possible only in a nation where the continuous inability to reach a final destination is the most compelling reason to keep setting out.

"It is not enough to affirm my liberty by choosing 'something,'" wrote Thomas Merton. "I must choose something *good.*" I choose a new kind of human society that generates a new kind of human being, committed to a universalist standard of one right, one law, one nation for all. I choose the greatest, freest, most generous nation in existence. I choose something good. *America.*

ACKNOWLEDGMENTS

When I began work on this book I didn't stop to consider that the process of writing it would reintroduce my psyche to so many individuals—friends, allies, adversaries, mentors, colleagues, and assorted passersby—who in various ways have influenced my personal and intellectual development over the more than four decades of experience that the book covers. I'm tempted to gratefully call the roll, but the scope of my appreciations would probably force my publisher to cut me off in midsentence like an actor who goes on too long at an awards ceremony. Instead I'll join the simpler sentiments of Ralph Waldo Emerson: "I awoke this morning with devout thanksgiving for my friends, the old and the new."

Special thanks to Ken Wilber, Bert Parlee, and Michael Ostrolenk for their thoughtful responses to my scattershot ruminations and declarations before I began writing specifically on the themes of *Leaving the Left*. My longtime friend and compatriot Peter Rojcewicz painstakingly reviewed an early overview of the book and offered many insightful suggestions and encouragement. Phil Cousineau has been a fellow traveler on too many intellectual voyages to name them all; his early audience for my ideas inspired me to go forward. Enormous gratitude goes to Lucianne Goldberg and Joni Evans for their wise counsel on how to translate my *San Francisco Chronicle* essay into a book.

My extraordinary editor, Bernadette Malone, understood and supported the book's core concept from the very beginning and kept faith with the project at every stage. I also thank Jillian Gray, Shannon Garrison, Will Weisser, Branda Maholtz, Bruce Giffords, and Rachel Burd for making it such a pleasure to work with Sentinel.

I'm deeply grateful to the many who sent messages of support in response to my *Chronicle* essay. Their marvelous spirit of community bolstered me at every stage of this book. And let me also thank the hateful American leftists who wrote to offer creative suggestions for anatomical possibilities (yoga postures?) that I might want to pursue alone, and the interesting travel ideas for very warm metaphysical terrains. I cannot begin to say I comprehend why so many of them hate their country and work so vigorously for its destruction, but I can say without hesitation that I am honored by their disdain for my work.

My most important work is as a father. Realizing that his writer dad had a lot to do in relation to something called deadlines, my son, Skyler, spent a lot of productive hours with colored pencils and drawing paper so I could stay on track. I adore him and am truly blessed.

Finally, I salute America's founders. Thanks to their foresight and willingness to put everything on the line, we are the strongest, freest, and most thriving nation on the face of the earth. "A Republic, if you can keep it," declared Ben Franklin in 1787. May we have the courage and stamina to keep on keeping America free.

NOTES

Complete publication data for works cited below appears in the bibliography.

PREFACE

viii *"I may be well dressed":* D'Souza, p. 102.
viii *And Gloria Steinem:* Schweizer, pp. 191–200.
viii *especially her cross-country travels:* A. Moore, 2003.

INTRODUCTION

xviii *Kafka, without the bug:* Kafka, 1972.
xviii *Think Kuhnian paradigm shift:* Kuhn, 1970.
 xix *"There is," said an Italian philosopher:* Kennedy, 1966.
xxiii *Susan Sontag cleared her throat:* Sontag, p. 76.
xxiii *Norman Mailer pronounced the dead:* Mailer, pp. E17–20.
xxiii *The events of that day were likely premeditated:* Vidal, pp. 14–17.
xxiii *Noam Chomsky insisted that al Qaeda:* Collier and Horowitz, pp. 169–70.
xxiii *In the name of diversity, the University of Arizona:* Sykes, p. 166.
xxiii *The University of Connecticut:* Ibid.
xxiii *Brown University:* Ibid, pp. 169–71.
xxiv *When actor Bill Cosby . . . "Where you is":* Cosby.
xxiv *speaking in the name of his blackness:* Dyson, pp. 33–43.
xxiv *"formerly poor black multimillionaire":* Dyson, p. 5.
xxiv *"lofty goal of proving that blacks are human":* Dyson, p. 20.
xxiv *"his duties as a racial representative":* Dyson, p. 3.
xxiv *"I should be able to get drunk at a fraternity party":* Paglia, p. 57.

xxiv   *Susan Estrich countered:* Sykes, p. 190.

xxv   *"that the ever renewing society will be a free society":* Blue and Savary, p. 163.

CHAPTER 1: RACISM IN THE NAME OF EQUALITY

1   *"four little children will one day live in a nation":* King, 1963.

3   *It has ruled that "Congress was intent":* Levin, p. 91.

4   *"You guys have been practicing discrimination for years":* Ibid., p. 89.

9   *"I will eat the pages of the civil rights bill":* Thernstrom and Thernstrom, 1999, p. 425.

10   *"Undeserved inequalities call for redress":* Rawls, p. 102.

10   *"Two great, immutable forces have driven America's attitudes":* Steele.

11   *"Implicit in this phrase is the coalescing of minorities":* Thernstrom and Thernstrom, 2002, p. 418.

11   *Writing in* Public Interest *in 1985:* Wilson.

13   *Philosopher Ken Wilber calls this "the philosophy of 'oops.'":* Wilber 2000(b), p. 3.

17   *"The first man, who after enclosing a piece of ground":* Horowitz, p. 145.

17   *Former leftist David Horowitz eloquently declares:* Ibid., p. 146.

18   *In his book* The Quest for Cosmic Justice: Sowell.

19   *a 640-pound contractor demanded:* Sykes, p. 7.

19   *Meanwhile, a Chicago man complained:* Ibid.

20   *"Once standing, this young man smiled":* Steele, p.76.

CHAPTER 2: THE GREAT CUYAHOGA LAND GRAB

28   *"He says we'll send armed men and take it away from you":* Frontline: For the Good of All. Producers: Mark Jury, Dan Jury, Stephanie Tepper. WGBH Boston, producer. Boston: WGBH Educational Foundation; June 6, 1983.

28   *Leonard Stein-Sapir was first told:* Ibid.

30   *"Ninety days is not nearly enough time":* Ibid.

30   *"The flower shop itself is a commercial operation":* Ibid.

35   *Mr. Chairman and distinguished senators . . . the central California coast:* Author's testimony to the national parks subcommittee of the U.S. Senate Committee on Energy and Natural Resources.

39   *Under the Supreme Court's 2005* Kelo v. New London *decision:* Kelo v. New London (04-108) 268 Conn. 1, 843 A. 2d 500; O'Connor, J., dissenting.

40 *"Now is the time for"*: "Grassroots Groundswell Grows Against Eminent Domain Abuse," Institute for Justice online statement, July 12, 2005.

41 *"What's been passed so far"*: "One Year After *Kelo* Argument National Property Rights Revolt Still Going Strong," Institute for Justice, February 21, 2006, www.ij.org/private_property/connecticut/2_21_06pr.html.

42 *"These private groups . . . one person at a time"*: Private communication with the author.

CHAPTER 3: "THIS BEGINS TO LOOK LIKE SICKNESS"

43 *"We ask no better laws . . . which your present laws secure to you"*: Dubois, p. 51.

44 *any theory of a unique "woman's vantage point" . . . "vast majority of women"*: Sykes, p. 180.

44 *"Marriage as an institution . . . of, or ownership"*: Dworkin.

44 *"A convention to discuss . . . at 10 o'clock A.M."*: Rossi, p. 413.

45 *These were "childless women," . . . "in their own flesh"*: Ibid., p. 414.

45 *When, in the course of human events . . . impel them to such a course:* Ibid., p. 415.

46 *He has never permitted her . . . and to administer chastisement:* Ibid., p. 416.

47 *As I was walking down a sleazy . . . and "Mama" took my place:* Rabuzzi, p. 1.

47 *It is a fine spring day . . . a ritual of subjugation:* Bartky, p. 27.

48 *"graduation from hell"*: Wolf, May 31, 1992.

48 *"There we were, . . . the choking silence, the complicity, the helplessness."* Ibid.

48 *"Is it possible . . . for them anyway?"* Sommers, p. 28.

49 *Earlier in this century . . . male's offensive coarseness:* Ibid., p. 29.

50 *"in this country alone . . . about 150,000 females die of anorexia each year"*: Steinem, p. 222.

50 *"How," she asks, "would America react"*: Wolf, 1992, pp. 180–82.

50 *"seek to demonstrate . . . by objectifying their bodies"*: Brumberg, pp. 19–20.

51 *"We were misquoted"*: Sommers, p. 12.

51 *One clinician told her that of 1,400 patients:* Ibid.

51 *"The deaths of these young women are a tragedy"*: Ibid.

51 *Ann Landers repeated it in her syndicated column:* Ibid.

51 *"Will she actually state" . . . "as Jews identify the death camps' "*: Ibid.

52   *"In a patriarchal society . . . strong enough to give consent":* Patai and Koertge.

53   *She finds that in no known:* Chafetz, p.21.

53   *Nor in any known society:* Ibid.

53   *"women's activities are either . . . relative equal status":* Ibid.

53   *"why are women nowhere . . . valued societal resources":* Ibid.

53   *"the women carry babies . . . their physical mobility":* Ibid., p. 22.

53   *"[I]n fact, for most human . . . been far from minimal":* Ibid.

54   *"most societies [to] find . . . no longer nursing":* Ibid.

54   *"on the basis of expediency . . . of breast-feeding":* Ibid.

54   *"in all the history . . . sphere of activity":* Ibid.

54   *[Speculative oppression] theories . . . of clear insight:* Ibid., p. 3.

56   *"Forget what you've heard about domestic violence":* Pearson, www. deltabravo.net/custody/fem-abusers.php

56   *The largest and most recent survey:* National Institute of Justice.

56   *"If you take into account":* Interview with the author.

56   *as was a book with coauthor Suzanne Steinmetz, Ph.D., in 1980:* Straus, Gelles, Steinmetz, 1980.

56–57 *Straus and Gelles reworked their questions:* Straus, Gelles, 1988.

57   *"In the rare instances" . . . "violence against women":* Author interview.

58   *"Feminist leaders deserve real credit for rallying" . . . "self-defense or the evils of patriarchy":* All David Fontes quotes are from interviews with the author.

59   *"These women were not . . . specific generalizations":* Walker.

59   *In a report called "Violent Touch: Breaking Through the Stereotypes":* Fontes.

59   *Dias identified domestic violence:* All Claudia Dias quotes are from interviews with the author.

61   *"No one is stating the obvious" . . . "taking this on as a men's problem":* Carol Delaney, "Crimes are by males," letter to the *San Francisco Chronicle* published August 5, 2002.

62   *"Women commit the majority . . . spousal assaults":* Pearson, p. 7.

62   *A study by the National Child Abuse and Neglect Data System:* National Child Abuse and Neglect Data System.

62   *"Female parents were identified . . . highest percentage of child victims":* U.S. Department of Health and Human Services.

62   *Washington state human services professional:* Lipshires.

63   *"as if half the population":* Pearson, p. 7.

64   *"I have to recant":* Pearson, 26.

64   *"The New Feminism emphasizes":* Holtby, 42.

CHAPTER 4: THE FALL AND RISE OF CLARENCE THOMAS

67 *"I was petrified by having . . . to destroy you as a person":* Danforth, p. 8.

67 *"We're going to Bork him . . . Where did he come from?":* Fund.

68 *"This had to be fought beyond the walls . . . and then we would lose":* Eastland.

68 *Thomas remembered riding in a car as a boy . . . WELCOMES YOU TO NORTH CAROLINA:* Danforth, p. 10.

68 *congresswoman Eleanor Holmes Norton . . . if he was going to sound like a white:* Charen.

69 *Derrick Bell of Harvard Law School opined . . . "black":* Puddington.

69 *Judge Bruce White of New York:* Ibid.

69 *Congressman Charles Rangel . . . "the interests of minorities":* Ibid.

69 *Judge Leon Higginbotham . . . "afflicted with racial self-hatred":* Troy.

69 *Columbia professor Manning Marable . . . "ceased being an African-American":* Peterson, p. 21.

69 *Carl Rowan: "If you give Thomas":* Ibid.

69 *Juan Williams wrote: . . . "the Leadership Conference on Civil Rights":* Williams.

70 *Thomas confided at the time:* Danforth, p. 150.

70 *On September 16, Melissa Riley . . . "Soviet Union":* Ibid., p. 29.

71 *Lee Liberman thought this was at least strange . . . " 'guy who harassed me to Job B' ":* Ibid., p. 31.

71 *"You've got to be kidding me" . . . "kind of charge . . . from which I can't clear myself":* Ibid., p. 34.

72 *"She was certainly not a Republican," . . . "very ideological":* Ibid., p. 136.

72 *first reaction to Hill's charges:* Ibid., p. 37.

72 *Diane Holt, remembers Hill, . . . and "pouting. . . . have the last say":* Ibid.

73 *Thomas dismisses this as "nonsense":* Ibid., p. 38.

73 *Thomas says that both . . . him to that position.* Ibid.

73 *Diane Holt says that . . . Hill denied making these statements:* Ibid.

73 *Armstrong Williams . . . "child accusing me of something":* Ibid., pp. 38–39.

75 *"I was harassed and I nipped it in the bud" . . . "Wouldn't you haul off and poke a guy in the mouth if he spoke in that manner?":* "Women See Hearing from a Perspective of Their Own Jobs," *New York Times,* October 18, 1991.

76 *Mr. Chairman, Senator Thurmond, members of the committee: . . . but it is too high:* Hearings.

80   *I think that this is a travesty . . . you will be lynched, destroyed, caricatured by a committee of the U.S. Senate, rather than hung from a tree:* Hearings.

CHAPTER 5: THE RIGHT TO KILL NEWBORNS

82   *"If that baby at twenty-four weeks was delivered accidentally" . . . Lautenberg said:* U.S. Senate debate, September 26, 1996.

83   *"My question is this," Santorum said, . . . floor of the Senate":* Ibid.

86   *Kate O'Beirne calls "the smallest humans,":* O'Beirne, p. 156.

87   *Blackmun wrote, "With respect . . . point is at viability":* Roe v. Wade.

88   *"The Roe framework, then, is clearly on a collision course":* Akron v. Akron Center for Reproductive Health, 462 U.S. 416 (1983), www. caselaw.lp.findlaw.com/scripts/getcase.pl?court-us.vivol-416.

88   *[T]he Court holds . . . choice after that time:* Epstein, p. 184.

89   *"One of the most curious . . . is nowhere to be found":* Tribe, 1973.

89   *Or Edward Lazarus, . . . Roe on its own terms":* Lazarus.

89   *Watergate special prosecutor . . . part of the Constitution":* Cox, pp. 113–14.

90   *"Roe, I believe, . . . not resolved, conflict":* Ginsburg.

90   *At the heart of the . . . to exterminate it:* Roe v. Wade.

CHAPTER 6: NONE DARE CALL IT PERJURY

96   *According to the* Wall Street Journal: Lyons.

96   *"That allegation," he replied:* Ibid.

96   *In a subsequent ABC . . . and his wife:* Ibid.

97   *You had a rap singer . . . I haven't met them:* CNN Specials.

98   *Now I have to . . . American people:* Harris and Balz.

99   *"It depends on what . . . accurate statement":* Clinton Grand Jury Testimony, September 21, 1998.

99   *This led his questioner . . . "literally true?":* Ibid.

99   *When Clinton was asked to explain . . . "thought we were":* Ibid.

99   *"With . . . one admission, . . . it's about sex":* Bennett, p. 13.

100   Washington Post *columnist . . . " 'misdemeanors' ":* Ibid.

100   *Geraldo Rivera said . . . "Get over it?":* Olasky, 1998.

100   *Democratic Party operative . . . "balancing the budget?":* Estrich, January 23, 1998.

100   *Social critic Wendy Kaminer, . . . "matter to voters?":* Bennett, p. 14.

100   *High-profile lawyer . . . "panty raid":* Ibid., p. 16.

100   *"These people . . . It's about sex":* Carville.

102   *To hear the boomeritis version, . . . (to the entire world):* Wilber, 2000(b), p. 18.

103   *Harvard philosopher Michael J. Sandal ... "public responsibilities":* Bennett, p. 15.

103   *"He plants a story, ... fornicators out of town":* Raasch.

104   *"If there is semen ... with the judge":* Hannity, p. 253.

104   *about "the time that this ... in the right direction":* Bennett, p. 32.

104   *Radcliffe College fellow ... "demagogues do":* Ibid.

105   *Today I am an inquisitor.... the Constitution:* Jordan.

107   *"We know very few facts":* Goldberg.

107   *"There are facts, ... thrown out of court":* Bennett, pp. 93–94.

107   *"If there is a privilege ... conversations with reporters":* Ibid., p. 94.

108   *"Because there's an investigation ... he can't":* Hines.

108   *"Drag a hundred-dollar bill":* Olson, p. 295.

108   *"God, no".... "you have to tell the truth":* Bennett, p. 128.

109   *"I want to say again ... the American people":* "Clinton apologizes to nation," CNN.com, February 12, 1999.

109   *Professor Hadley Arkes ... " 'what is the problem?' ":* Arkes.

109   *"There's no one left to lie to":* Baker, Eilperin.

CHAPTER 7: COLUMBINE CALLING AMERICA

111   *Many pundits on air ... attention, involvement, and attitude:* Smith, 1999.

113   *"in grade school knew ... enters the room":* Bly, p. 3.

113   *"All the parents" ... "possibilities formerly shut off by that 'control system' ":* Bly, p. 3.

114   *A northern California mother ... "to get an education":* Telephone interview with the author, March 18, 2003.

115   *The baby boomers are a generation ... for spoiling childhood:* Ibid.

115   *"The structure of the workplace ... raise children today":* Ibid.

115   *"Our generation came up" ... "they've done something wrong":* Kindlon, p. 13.

117   *"The same forces ... by emptying them":* Hymowitz, p. xii.

118   *"About 12 percent ... did community service":* Interview with the author, April 6, 2002.

118   *"In many ways," ... "a yellow submarine":* Bly, p. 44.

119   *"it is hard to know ... where your children are":* Ibid., p. xiii.

119   *"So many parents are":* All Elise Webster quotes are from interviews with the author.

120   *"The word discipline":* All Bonnie Romanow quotes are from interviews with the author."

121   *Such parents "vacillate wildly" ... "lens of their own needs":* Ehrensaft, p. 46.

122   *"She never had"* ... *"Age isn't an issue for her": People* magazine, April 19, 2002, www.people.aol.com/people/articles/0,19736,623873,00.html.

122   *"Who am I doing this for, me or my child'?":* Ehrensaft, p. 240.

123   *What is asked ... The parents have to know that:* Bly, p. 237.

CHAPTER 8: BLAMING AMERICA FIRST

125   *continuing to serve ... how could the reports be refuted?:* Collier and Horowitz, p. x.

126   *In 1970, Chomsky ... "a model for themselves":* Chomsky, 1970.

126   *He compared those killed ... whatever happened in Cambodia:* Collier and Horowitz, p. x.

127   *In October 2003, ... "but Cuba has always been in him":* Lagarde.

127   *During his 2003 visit, ... "five patriotic Cuban prisoners":* Ibid.

127   *The terrorist attacks ... no one cares to pursue it:* Available at www.zmag.org.

128   *"What has the United States done":* Hacker.

128   *America is "an imperialist nation":* Greene.

128   *"This is a case of the chickens":* Barsamian.

128   *At Marquette University:* Kirby.

128   *Residence hall directors ... "were offending people":* Francetic.

128   *Cafeteria supervisors ... so they took it down:* Flynn, p. 18.

128   *Florida Gulf Coast University's ... "standards of civility and tolerance":* Flynn, p. 18.

129   *Margaret Post, ... "in which this occurred":* Ibid., p. 19.

129   *"The* New York Times *headline"... "trying to keep them down":* Dryer and Ferraro.

129   *University of Massachusetts–Amherst ... "of American policy":* Israel.

129   *Professor Robert Jensen ... "committed in my lifetime":* Jensen.

129   *American University professor ... view of history:* Flynn, p. 20.

130   *University of New Mexico ... to his next class:* Barron.

131   *"What is so heartbreaking ... misogynist ideology":* Neumann.

132   *"the wholesale massacres ... religious and 'fundamentalist' forms":* Sullivan.

135   *"Feelings of guilt":* Barfield, p. 58.

135   *"glad":* www.abcnews.go.com/ThisWeek/Politics/story?id=1880310&page=1.

137   *"be clear about why ... for their actions":* Rushdie.

138   *"soft on crime and soft on fascism":* Hitchens.

138   *NAACP issued an equally ... "none of us is safe":* Sullivan.

138   *When Senator Ted Kennedy:* Sammon, p. 51.

138 *"Iraqis who have risen up . . . and they will win":* Moore, M.

140 *"so many Muslims are eager . . . career opportunity":* Harris, S., p. 32.

141 *I am colored:* www.xroads.virginia.edu/~MA01/Grand-Jean/Hurston/ Chapters/how.html.

CHAPTER 9: DISPLACED DADS

148 *In the wake of that legal ruling* (Marriage of LaMusga): *In re Marriage of LaMusga* (2004) 32 C.4th 1072.

148 *When the California Supreme Court: In re Marriage of Burgess* (1996) 13 C.4th 25.

148 *feminist California Women's Law Center:* McKee.

148 *"This decision changes the focus" . . . "she wants to give up":* All Eric Traub quotes are from an interview with the author, San Rafael, Calif., May 24, 2004.

149 *"This area of law . . . cases before them":* In re Marriage of LaMusga (2004) 32 C.4th 1072.

149 *"the likely impact . . . a change in custody":* Ibid.

150 *Leslie Shear, . . . "an absolute victory for the children":* McKee.

150 *No way, . . . "toward an ex-spouse":* Ibid.

151 *Garrett Dailey, . . . his court-ordered visitation:* All Garrett Dailey quotes are from an interview with author, May 26, 2004, by telephone.

151 *In its La Musga ruling . . . "'communication with him as possible'":* In re Marriage of LaMusga (2004) 32 C.4th 1072.

154 *Wallerstein's brief emphasized . . . "psychological development":* Interview with the author, May 28, 2004, by telephone.

154 *Richard Warshak, . . . warrants stability and continuity:* Brief of Amici Curiae On Behalf of Minor Children Re: *In re the Marriage of Susan Poston Navarro (LaMusga) and Gary LaMusga.* www.thelizlibrary.org/ lamusga/submittedWarshakamicibrief.pdf

155 *"We know now that children" . . . otherwise toxic in their influence, Kelly adds:* All Kelly quotes are from an interview with the author, June 1, 2004, by telephone.

156 *"Fathers and husbands own" . . . "It's crazy":* Quinn.

157 *In a recent ruling: Brown v. Yana* 2d Civil No. B170252 (Super. Ct. No. DR 21998).

157 *In "Deconstructing the Essential Father," . . . "married family":* Silverstein and Auerbach.

158 *"Controlling for factors" . . . article entitled "Discovering What Families Can Do":* O'Beirne, pp. 12–13.

159 *the value I place on family diversity:* Council on Family Law.

159 *"if the people whom you live with":* O'Beirne, p. 5.
160 *"The father has lost his prestige":* Badinter, p. 130.
160 *"mothers are discounted everywhere":* Bly, p. 230.
160 *A society in which women are alone:* http://www.townhall.com/opinion/columns/kathleenparker/2006/03/22/190780.html.

CHAPTER 10: KILLING FOR CONVENIENCE

162 *Schiavo said: "Because":* Larry King Live, CNN, March 18, 2005.
162 *"Have you considered"* ... *"I will remain guardian":* "Terri's Death Wish or Michael's?" WorldNetDaily.com, March 20, 2005.
162 *"Yes, I do.":* Larry King Live, CNN, March 18, 2005.
165 *The Oregon law "is the latest result"* ... *"take a quicker way out,":* Hendin.
165 *Dutch physician Richard Fenigsen* ... *eighty thousand to three hundred thousand cases per year:* Fenigsen.
166 *Health Minister Els Borst:* "Dutch 'Mercy Killing Law' Passed," *BBC News*, April 11, 2001.
166 *"Dutch doctors who practice"* ... *"the Dutch reality":* Fenigsen.
167 *From our point of view* ... *about their data?:* Hendin.
167 *"There is considerable* ... *the right to live":* Fenigsen.
167 *Fenigsen notes that* ... *"of the physician provocateur":* Ibid.
169 *Pro-life feminist* ... *"nor for physicians":* Callahan.
169 *Self-knowledge is difficult* ... *"act of self-extinction?:* Ibid.
170 *"yet would never think* ... *considered morally significant":* Singer, 2005.
171 *A reporter for* Vegan Voice ... *"beings to some extent":* "Is This a Dangerous Philosopher?" *Vegan*, Issue No. 8, December 2001–February 2002.
171 *"would allow parents and doctors":* Nasar.
172 *"I propose to use [the term]* ... *experiencing pleasure and pain, etc.:* Singer, 1993, p. 87.
172 *"What about parents conceiving"* ... *"really wrong in itself":* Olasky, 2004.
172 *Is there anything wrong* ... *"No," Singer responded:* Ibid.
172 *"We protest his hiring* ... *protection against homicide":* Princeton Students.
173 *In his book* The Expanding Circle ... *"saving specific, identifiable lives":* Colossi.
173 *the difference, when the sufferer:* http://www.godspy.com/issues/WHATS-LOVE-GOT-TO-DO-WITH-IT-The-Ethical-Contradictions-of-Peter-Singer-by-Dr-Peter-J-Colosi.cfm.

174   *"There was also a dark side," . . . "appendix from a diseased body"*: Gallagher.
175   *"In Oregon," . . . "its own death knell"*: Physicians for Compassionate Care, www.pccef.org.
176   *"Habituation makes each new case . . . as his first case"*: Callahan.

AFTERWORD

180   *"Liberals see inequality"*: Limbaugh.
180   *"An atavistic longing . . . collectivist tradition"*: Hayek, pp. 133–34.
181   *"women can't be . . . for any reason"*: O'Beirne, p. 157.
181   *"the moral test . . . and the handicapped"*: Humphrey.
182   *"inability to come . . . an earthly redemption"*: Horowitz, 2003.
182   *our political lexicon . . . or a Republican:* Medcalf.
183   *"It is not enough . . . choose something good"*: Blue and Savary, p. 187.

BIBLIOGRAPHY

Akron v. Akron Center for Reproductive Health, 462 U.S. 416 (1983).

Arkes, Hadley. "The Bully Pulpiteer—Pres. Clinton's Character," *National Review,* September 2, 1996.

Badinter, Elizabeth. *The Unopposite Sex: The End of the Gender Battle.* Translated by Barbara Wright. New York: Harper and Row, 1989.

Baker, Peter, and Juliet Eilperin, "Debate on Impeachment Opens," *Washington Post,* December 11, 1992, p. A1.

Barfield, Owen. *History, Guilt, and Habit.* Middletown, Conn.: Wesleyan University Press, 1979.

Barron, James. "Professor 'Sorry' for Pentagon Remark." *Daily Lobo,* September 24, 2001, p. 1.

Barsamian, David. Quoted in Jessika Fruchter, "Peace Community Speaks Out Against War," *Colorado Daily,* September 18, 2001, p. 4.

Bartky, Sandra Lee. *Femininity and Domination: Studies in the Phenomenology of Oppression.* New York: Routledge, 1990.

Bennett, William J. *The Death of Outrage: Bill Clinton and the Assault on American Ideals.* New York: The Free Press, 1998.

Blackmun, Harry. *Regents of the University of California v. Bakke,* 438 U.S. 265, 407 (1978).

Blue, Adrianne, and Louis M. Savary. *Faces of Freedom.* Winona, Minnesota: St. Mary's College Press, 1969.

Bly, Robert. *The Sibling Society.* New York: Vintage, 1997.

Brumberg, Joan Jacobs. *Fasting Girls: The Emergence of Anorexia Nervosa as a Modern Disease.* Cambridge, MA: Harvard University Press, 1988.

Callahan, Sydney. "A Feminist Case Against Self-Determined Dying in Assisted Suicide and Euthanasia." *Studies in Prolife Feminism,* vol. 1, issue 4, September 22, 1995.

Carville, James. *Good Morning America* (ABC television broadcast, February 26, 1998).

Chafetz, Janet Saltzman. *Sex and Advantage.* Totowa, NJ: Rowman & Alanheld, 1984.

Charen, Mona. "This Nomination Is Not a Quota Filler," *Newsday*, July 10, 1991.

Chomsky, Noam. Speech delivered on April 13, 1970, in Hanoi while visiting North Vietnam. Radio Hanoi broadcast the speech on April 14, and Chomsky's address was published in the *Asia-Pacific Daily Report*, Foreign Broadcast Information Service, April 16, 1970, pp. K2–K3.

Churchill, Ward. "Some People Push Back: On the Justice of Roosting Chickens," *Pockets of Resistance* no. 11, September 12, 2001, www. orlandodirectaction.us/churchill.html.

Clinton Grand Jury Testimony, *USA Today*, September 21, 1998.

CNN Specials. "Bill Clinton 1992: Road to the White House," www.cnn.com/ SPECIALS/multimedia/timeline/9809/start.report/cnn.content/ clinton.92.

Collier, Peter, and David Horowitz, eds. *The Anti-Chomsky Reader.* San Francisco: Encounter Books, 2004.

Colossi, Peter. "What's Love Got to Do with It?" *Godspy: Faith at the Edge,* April 4, 2006.

Cosby, Bill. Address at the NAACP's Gala to Commemorate the 50th Anniversary of *Brown v. Board of Education.* Washington, D.C., May 17, 2004.

Council on Family Law, "The Future of Family Law: Law and the Marriage Crisis in North America," Institute for American Values, p. 17.

Cox, Archibald. *The Role of the Supreme Court in American Government.* New York: Oxford University Press, 1977, pp. 113–14.

Danforth, John C. *Resurrection: The Confirmation of Clarence Thomas.* New York: Viking, 1994.

Dryer, Zander, and Matthew Ferraro. "Where Does America Go from Here?" *Yale Herald,* September 14, 2001, p. 3.

D'Souza, Dinesh. *What's So Great About America?* New York: Penguin, 2002.

Dubois, Ellen Carol, ed. *The Elizabeth Cady Stanton–Susan B. Anthony Reader.* Boston: Northeastern University Press, 1992.

Dworkin, Andrea. *Letters from a War Zone.* New York: Dutton, 1989.

Dyson, Michael Eric. *Is Bill Cosby Right?* New York: Basic Civitas Books, 2005.

Eastland, Terry. "Bork Revisited." *Commentary,* February 1990.

Ehrensaft, Diane. *Spoiling Childhood: How Well-Meaning Parents Are Giving*

Children Too Much—But Not What They Need. New York: Guilford Press, 1999.

Epstein, Richard A. "Substantive Due Process by Any Other Name: The Abortion Cases," in Philip B. Kurland, et al., *The Supreme Court Review, 1973* (Chicago: University of Chicago Press, 1974).

Estrich, Susan. "Matt, Bill, and Monica." *Slate,* January 23, 1998.

Fenigsen, Richard. "A Case Against Dutch Euthanasia." Hastings Center Report, Garrison, New York: January 1, 1989.

Flynn, Daniel L. *Why the Left Hates America: Exposing the Lies That Have Obscured America's Greatness.* New York: Forum Books, 2002.

Fontes, David. "Violent Touch: Breaking Through the Stereotypes," 1998 and 2003. www.safe4all.org/essays/vtbreak.pdf.

Francetic, Tony. "University May Be Infringing on Students' Rights." *Central Michigan Life,* October 10, 2001, p. 1.

Fund, John. "The Borking Begins." *Opinion Journal,* January 8, 2001, www.opinionjournal.com/diary/?id-85000412.

Gallagher, Hugh. "What the Nazi 'Euthanasia Program' Can Tell Us About Disability Oppression." *Journal of Disability Policy Studies,* September 22, 2001.

Ginsburg, Ruth Bader. "Some Thoughts on Autonomy and Equality in Relation to *Roe v. Wade.*" 63 *North Carolina Law Review,* 375 (1985), 382.

Goldberg, Jonah. "Spinning Wheels." *National Review,* October 12, 1998.

Greene, Joshua. "Forget the Media and See the Truth." *Daily Athenaeum,* September 13, 2001, p. 4.

Hacker, Christopher. "Why Is the Bigger Question." *Badger Herald,* September 13, 2001.

Hannity, Sean. *Let Freedom Ring: Winning the War of Liberty over Liberalism.* New York: ReganBooks, 2002.

Harris, John F., and Don Balz. "Clinton Forcefully Denies Affair, or Urging Lies." *Washington Post,* January 27, 1998; page A-1.

Harris, Sam. *The End of Faith: Religion, Terror, and the Future of Reason.* New York: W. W. Norton, 2004.

Hayek, F. A. *The Mirage of Social Justice.* Chicago: The University of Chicago Press, 1978.

Hearings Before the Committee on the Judiciary of the United States Senate, 102d Cong., 1st sess., on the nomination of Clarence Thomas to be associate justice of the Supreme Court of the United States.

Hendin, Herbert. "Assisted Suicide and Euthanasia: Oregon Tries the Dutch Way." *Psychiatric Times,* vol. XII, issue 4 (April 1995).

Hendin, Herbert, et al. "Physician-Assisted Suicide and Euthanasia in the

Netherlands: Lessons from the Dutch." *Journal of the American Medical Association,* vol. 277, no. 21 (June 4, 1997), p. 1721.

Hines, Cragg. "Hillary Clinton takes defender-in-chief role." *Houston Chronicle,* January 28, 1998.

Hitchens, Christopher. "Of Sin, the Left & Islamic Fascism." *The Nation,* October 8, 2001.

Holtby, Winifred. "Feminism Divided." *Modern Feminism,* ed. Maggie Humm. New York: Columbia University Press, 1992.

Horowitz, *David. Left Illusions: An Intellectual Odyssey.* Dallas: Spence Publishing Company, 2003.

_____.*The Politics of Bad Faith.* New York: Touchstone, 1998.

Humphrey, Hubert H. Remarks at Democratic National Convention, New York, July 13, 1976.

Hymowitz, Kay. *Liberation's Children: Parents and Kids in a Postmodern Age.* Chicago: Ivan R. Dee, 2003.

Israel, Bill. "A Policy of Neglect and Cowardice, a Pay-Off of Death." *Massachusetts Daily Collegian,* September 13, 2001, p. 6.

Jensen, Robert. "U.S. Just as Guilty of Committing Own Violent Acts." *Houston Chronicle,* September 14, 2001, p. 33.

Jordan, Barbara. Statement on the Articles of Impeachment, delivered June 25, 1974, U.S. House of Representatives Judiciary Committee.

Kafka, Franz. *The Metamorphosis.* New York: Bantam Classics, 1972.

Kennedy, Robert F. "Day of Affirmation" address delivered in Capetown, South Africa, June 6, 1966.

Kindlon, Daniel J. *Too Much of a Good Thing: Raising Children of Character in an Indulgent Age.* New York: Miramax Books, 2003.

King, Martin Luther, Jr. "I Have a Dream" address delivered in Washington, D.C., August 28, 1963.

Kirby, Adam S. "College Republicans Barred from Holding Memorial Event." *Marquette Tribune,* September 12, 2001, p. 1.

Kuhn, Thomas S. *The Structure of Scientific Revolutions.* Chicago: University of Chicago Press, 1970.

Lagarde, M. H. "Cuba Always Has Been with Him." *La Jiribila* [Cuba], no. 129.

Lazarus, Edward. "The Lingering Problems with *Roe v. Wade,* and Why the Recent Senate Hearings on Michael McConnell's Nomination Only Underlined Them." FindLaw Legal Commentary, FindLaw.com, Oct. 3, 2002.

Levin, Mark R. *Men in Black.* Washington, D.C.: Regnery Publishing, 2005.

Limbaugh, Rush. "What Is Conservatism?" Premium for subscribers to *The Limbaugh Letter.*

Lipshires, Lisa. "Female Perpetration of Child Sexual Abuse: An Overview of the Problem." *Moving Forward Newsjournal,* vol. 2, no. 6 (July/August, 1994), www.mensconfraternity.org.au/menswebpage97.html.

Lyons, Gene. "The Real-Life 'Primary Colors.'" *The Consortium,* www.consortiumnews.com/archive/clinto15.html. 1998.

McKee, Mike. "Divorced Parents Must Consider Ex if Moving Away." *The Recorder* (ALM Media), May 3, 2004.

Mailer, Norman. "America Is So Vain." (London) *Sunday Times,* September 8, 2002.

Medcalf, Jeff. "Party of the West." *Caerdroia: A Strange Loop,* 2005, www.caerdroia.org/blog/archives/2005/05/party_of_the_we.html.

Moore, Art. "High-living Celebs Tie SUV Owners to Terror." WorldNetDaily, January 10, 2003, www.worldnetdaily.com/news/article/asp?ARTICLE_ID-30412.

Moore, Michael. "Heads Up . . . from Michael Moore." Michaelmoore.com, April 14, 2004.

Nasar, Sylvia. "Princeton's New Philosopher Draws a Stir." *New York Times,* April 10, 1999.

National Child Abuse and Neglect Data System: Summary of Key Findings From Calendar Year 2000. Washington, DC: U.S. Department of Health and Human Resources. Administration for Children and Families.

National Institute of Justice and Centers for Disease Control and Prevention. "Prevalence, Incidence, and Consequences of Violence Against Women: Findings from the National Violence Against Women Survey," November 1998.

Neumann, Rachel. "The Empire Strikes Back: War vs. Peace: Novelists and Essayists Tell the 'Voice' Where They Stand." *Village Voice,* October 3–9, 2001, www.villagevoice.com/news/0140,neumann,28679,1.html.

O'Beirne, Kate. *Women Who Make the World Worse.* New York: Sentinel, 2006.

Olasky, Marvin. "Honor the King." *World Magazine,* May 23, 1998.

——. "Blue State Philosopher." *World Magazine,* November 27, 2004.

Olson, Barbara. *Hell to Pay: The Unfolding Story of Hillary Clinton.* Washington, D.C.: Regnery, 1999.

Paglia, Camille. *Sex, Art, and American Culture.* New York: Vintage Books, 1992.

Patai, Daphne, and Noretta Koertge. *Professing Feminism: Education and Indoctrination in Women's Studies.* Lanham, NY: Lexington Books, 2003.

Pearson, Patricia. *When She Was Bad: Violent Women and the Myth of Innocence.* New York: Viking, 1997.

Perazzo, John. "How the Left Trashes Black Conservatives." FrontPageMaga-zine.com, July 10, 2002.

Peterson, Jesse Lee. *Scam: How Black Leadership Exploits Black America.* Nashville: WND Books, 2003.

Princeton Students Against Infanticide. "Statement on the Hiring of Peter Singer." Princeton University, Princeton, NJ.

Quinn, Michelle. "Custody Law Shifts Away from Mothers." *San Jose Mercury News,* May 10, 2004, p. 1A.

Raasch, Chuck. "Carville Accuses Starr of Being Obsessed with 'Getting' Clinton," Gannett News Service, February 24, 1998.

Rabuzzi, Kathryn Allen. *Motherself: A Mythic Analysis of Motherhood.* Bloomington, IN: Indiana University Press, 1988.

Rawls, John. *A Theory of Justice.* Cambridge: Harvard University Press, 1971.

Roe v. Wade, 410 U.S. 113 (1973).

Rossi, Alice, ed. *The Feminist Papers: From Adams to de Beauvoir.* New York: Columbia University Press, 1993.

Rushdie, Salman. "Fighting the Forces of Invisibility." *Washington Post,* October 2, 2001, p. A25.

Sammon, Bill. *Strategy: How George W. Bush Is Defeating Terrorists, Outwitting Democrats, and Confounding the Mainstream Media.* Washington: Regnery, 2006.

Schweizer, Peter. *Do As I Say (Not As I Do).* New York: Doubleday, 2005.

Silverstein, L. B., and C. F. Auerbach. "Deconstructing the Essential Father." *American Psychologist* 54 (1999), 397–407.

Singer, Peter. *Practical Ethics.* Cambridge: Cambridge University Press, 1993.

Singer, Peter, ed. *In Defense of Animals: The Second Wave.* Malden, MA: Blackwell, 2005.

Smith, Susan Bitter. "Columbine's Lesson: Pay More Attention to Your Kids." *Arizona Republic,* April 30, 1999.

Sommers, Christina Hoff. *Who Stole Feminism?* New York: Simon and Schuster, 1994.

Sontag, Susan. "First Reactions." *The New Yorker.* September 24, 2001.

Sowell, Thomas. *The Quest for Cosmic Justice.* New York: Free Press, 2002.

Steele, Shelby. "The Age of White Guilt and the Disappearance of the Black Individual." *Harper's,* November 2002.

Steinem, Gloria. *Revolution from Within: A Book of Self-Esteem.* Boston: Little, Brown, 1992.

Straus, Murray A., Richard J. Gelles, Suzanne K. Steinmetz. *Behind Closed Doors: Violence in the American Family.* Garden City, NY: Anchor Press/Doubleday, 1980.

Straus, M. A., and R. J. Gelles. "How Violent Are American Families? Estimates from the National Family Violence Resurvey and Other Studies." In *Family Abuse and Its Consequences: New Directions in Research.* G. T. Hotaling, D. Finkelhor, J. T. Kirkpatrick, and M. A. Straus, eds. Newbury Park, CA: Sage Publications, 1988.

Sullivan, Andrew. "The Agony of the Left." *Wall Street Journal,* October 10, 2001.

Sykes, Charles J. *A Nation of Victims.* New York: St. Martin's Press, 1992.

Thernstrom, Stephan, and Abigail Thernstrom. *America in Black and White.* New York: Touchstone, 1999.

———. *Beyond the Color Line.* Stanford, CA: Hoover Institution Press, and New York: Manhattan Institute, 2002.

Thomas, Cal. "Feminists Complicit in Rape in America." *Austin American-Statesman,* February 27, 1999.

Tribe, Laurence H. "The Supreme Court, 1972 Term—Foreword: Toward a Model of Roles in the Due Process of Life and Law." 87 *Harvard Law Review* 1, 7 (1973), p. 46.

Troy, Daniel. "Law Review, Bar Brawl: The ABA Prepares to Fight Dirty." *National Review,* November 23, 1998.

U.S. Department of Health and Human Services, Administration on Children, Youth, and Families. "Child Maltreatment 1999." Washington, D.C.: 2001.

Vidal, Gore. "The Enemy Within." *The Observer,* October 27, 2002, review section.

Walker, Lenore E. *The Battered Woman.* New York: Harper & Row, 1979.

Wall Street Journal, "The Silent Scandal," May 25, 1982.

Wilber, Ken. *Sex, Ecology, Spirituality.* Boston: Shambhala Publications, Inc. 1995, 2000(a).

———. *The Collected Works of Ken Wilber, Vol. Seven.* Boston: Shambhala Books, 2000(b).

Williams, Juan. "Open Season on Clarence Thomas." *Washington Post,* October 10, 1991.

Wilson, James Q. "The Recovery of Character: Private Virtue and Public Policy." *The Public Interest,* no. 81 (Fall 1985).

Wolf, Naomi. "A Woman's Place." *New York Times,* May 31, 1992. Wolf's essay was a shortened version of a commencement speech she had just delivered to the Scripps College class of 1992.

———. *The Beauty Myth: How Images of Beauty Are Used Against Women.* New York: Doubleday, 1992.

INDEX